NATIONAL OCEANIC AND ATMOSPHERIC ADMINISTRATION

Scientific Diving Standards and Safety Manual

Revised
December 2011

FOREWORD

This document represents the minimum safety standards for scientific diving under the auspices of the National Oceanic and Atmospheric Administration (NOAA) as of the approval date of this Manual. As diving progresses so shall this standard and it is the responsibility of every NOAA diver to ensure that it continues to reflect the latest information on safe diving practices.

REVISION HISTORY

DATE: DESCRIPTION:
 August 15, 2008   Original document approved

APPROVALS:
OMAO Director   _____   12/16/2011
                                   RADM Jonathan W. Bailey, NOAA

NOAA Diving Control and Safety Board

Diving Program Manager   _____   November 2011
                                   David A. Dinsmore

Diving Safety Officer   _____   November 2011
                                   Steven C. Urick

NMFS Diving Officer   _____   November 2011
                                   Andrew W. David

NOS Diving Officer   _____   November 2011
                                   Greg B. McFall

OMAO Diving Officer   _____   November 2011
                                   Douglas R. Schleiger

OAR Diving Officer   Vacant at time of review   _____

NMFS Deputy Diving Officer   _____   November 2011
                                   Raymond Boland

NOS Deputy Diving Officer   _____   November 2011
                                   Mitchell Tartt

OMAO Deputy Diving Officer   _____   November 2011
                                   Bill J. Gordon

December 2011

TABLE OF CONTENTS

December 2011

SECTION 1:   ADMINISTRATION

1.1   General Provisions

1.1.1   Purpose.
   A. The purpose of the NOAA Scientific Diving Standards and Safety Manual (Manual) is to ensure all scientific diving is conducted in a manner that will maximize protection of scientific divers from accidental injury and/or illness, and to set forth standards for training and certification that will allow reciprocity with other science-oriented diving programs. Fulfillment of these purposes shall be consistent with the furtherance of scientific research and safety.
   B. This Manual sets minimum standards for the National Oceanic and Atmospheric Administration (NOAA) scientific diving operations, describes the organization for the conduct of scientific diving, and the basic standards and procedures for safety in scientific diving operations. It also establishes a framework for reciprocity between NOAA and other organizations that adhere to these standards.

1.1.2   Definition of Scientist and Scientist-In-Training. For the purposes of performing operational scientific dives, or scientific training and proficiency dives consistent with this Manual, divers must be one of the following:
   A. Scientist. An individual who utilizes scientific expertise to perform scientific dives without direct or indirect supervision or guidance from a more qualified individual as determined by the on-site Divemaster (DM)/Lead Diver (LD) and Chief Scientist.
   B. Scientist-In-Training. An individual who utilizes scientific expertise to perform scientific dives under the direct or indirect supervision or guidance of a scientist and approval of the on-site DM or LD.

1.1.3   OSHA Scientific Exemption.
   A. In 1982, The Occupational Safety and Health Administration (OSHA) exempted scientific diving from commercial diving regulations (Code of Federal Regulations, 29 CFR 1910, Subpart T) under certain conditions that are outlined below. The final guidelines for the exemption became effective in 1985 (Federal Register, Vol. 50, No.6, p.1046).
   B. Per 29 CFR 1910, Subpart T, "Scientific diving means diving performed solely as a necessary part of a scientific, research, or educational activity by employees whose sole purpose for diving is to perform scientific research tasks."
   C. Examples of scientific diving tasks include but are not limited to: data collection (water or bottom samples flora and fauna, etc.); observing and documenting (including the use of cameras); and measuring and counting. The tasks which can be completed by a scientific diver are limited to observation and data gathering and are performed for collection of data used for the advancement of science. If tools are used, they include but are not limited to "light" hand tools (e.g., small hammers, pliers, screw drivers, chisels). Other ancillary equipment such as small lift bags (≤100 pounds lifting capacity) and small air lifts can also be used if the tasks are associated with data collection. Tasks such as those described above performed by scientific divers are exempt from the OSHA commercial diving regulations found in 29 CFR 1910, Subpart T.
   D. Tasks, such as those involving ship husbandry (cleaning hulls, sea strainers, replacing zincs, un-fouling a ship's propeller); use of heavy power tools powered by pneumatics or hydraulics from the surface; lifting, positioning and retrieving heavy

objects; construction, underwater cutting or welding using exothermic cutting lances, and use of explosives cannot be conducted under the scientific exemption and as such are not covered in this Manual (refer to the NOAA Working Diving Standards and Safety Manual (NWDSSM)).

1.1.4   Scope and Application.
  A. The policies and procedures in this Manual apply to:
      1) All NOAA scientific diving operations regardless of where or when they are conducted;
      2) All NOAA employees engaged in scientific diving activities during official duty hours (i.e., when receiving financial compensation for work performed) where compressed gas is breathed in a hyperbaric environment; and
      3) Non-NOAA personnel performing scientific dives under the direct supervision of a NOAA DM or LD. For the purposes of this Manual, NOAA employees and non-NOAA personnel diving under the auspices of NOAA shall be collectively referred to as "NOAA divers."
  B. Working versus Scientific dives. Unit Diving Supervisors (UDS) or designee shall be responsible for determining whether dive operations are to be conducted per this Manual or the NOAA Working Diving Standards and Safety Manual based on review of the dive plan. Criteria to be used to distinguish between a working and scientific dive are presented at www.osha.gov and in the list below. A negative answer to any of the following questions would require the task to be conducted as a working dive following the standards outlined in this Manual.

Can the tasks be accomplished using simple hand tools (e.g., small hammers, pliers, chisels, wrenches, cameras, measuring tapes, nets, collection jars) weighing 25 pounds or less underwater?
Do the tasks require the expertise of a scientist or scientist-in-training?
Can the tasks be accomplished with minimal physical exertion?
Can the tasks be accomplished in short duration (e.g., <1-hour)?
Are the tasks limited solely to the observation of natural phenomena or responses of natural systems and/or gathering of data for scientific analysis?
If any object is to be lifted or moved, is its weight underwater <100 pounds?
Will the tasks result in the advancement of science?

  C. When conducting mixed operations (i.e., dives involving both scientific and working tasks), or when in doubt as to the nature of the dive, the dive shall be conducted as a working dive per the NWDSSM.

1.1.5   Obligations, Restrictions, and Conditions.
  A. The NOAA Diving Program (NDP) ensures all NOAA divers are in compliance with:
      1) All standards of general applicability outlined in 29 CFR Part 1910, Subpart T; and
      2) All policies and procedures outlined in this Manual.
  B. The NOAA Diving Control and Safety Board (NDCSB) may elect to implement and enforce more stringent diving standards and procedures than those stated herein. Such changes will be promulgated in writing to all affected employees and supervisors prior to implementation and will be included in the next revision to this Manual.

C. Failure to comply with the standards outlined in this Manual may be cause for the revocation or restriction of the diver's certification by action of the NDCSB.

D. No person shall engage in scientific diving operations under the auspices of the NDP unless they hold a current certification issued pursuant to the provisions of this Manual.

E. No dive team member shall be exposed to hyperbaric conditions against their will, except when necessary to prevent or treat a pressure-related injury.

F. No dive team member shall be permitted to dive with any known medical condition that is likely to adversely affect the safety and health of the diver or other dive team members.

1.1.6 Substitutions for Required Equipment, Materials, Apparatuses, Arrangements, Procedures, or Tests.

A. The NDCSB may accept substitutes for equipment, materials, apparatuses, arrangements, procedures, or tests required in this Manual if it can be demonstrated the substitutes provide an equivalent or increased level of safety.

B. Where it is shown to the satisfaction of the NDCSB that the use of any particular equipment, material, apparatus, arrangement, procedure, or test is unreasonable or impracticable, the NDCSB may permit the use of alternate equipment, material, apparatus, arrangement, procedure, or test to such an extent and upon such condition that insures, to the satisfaction of the NDCSB, a degree of safety consistent with the minimum standards set forth in this Manual.

C. Such changes will be codified in future revisions of this Manual and disseminated to all NOAA divers with an effective date of implementation.

1.1.7 Deviations in Emergencies.

A. NOAA divers may deviate from the requirements of this Manual provided that:
   1) The deviation is necessary to prevent or minimize a situation which is likely to cause death, serious physical harm, total loss of property, or major environmental damage; and
   2) The DM or LD notifies the NOAA Diving Program Manager (NDPM), UDS, and Line/Staff Office Diving Officers (LODO/SODO) of the deviation within 24 hours of the onset of the emergency situation.

B. The NDPM will in turn notify the Director, Office of Marine and Aviation Operations (OMAO), within 48 hours of the onset of the emergency situation indicating the nature of the emergency and extent of the deviation from the prescribed regulations.

1.1.8 Manual Revisions.

A. The NDCSB shall review this Manual at a minimum of every 2 years.

B. This Manual shall be:
   1) Issued, updated, and maintained by the NDP; and
   2) Distributed in paper or electronic form.

1.1.9 Reference Material.

A. A copy of this Manual, NOAA Administrative Order 209-123, all NOAA Diving Safety Bulletins, and the latest edition of the NOAA Diving Manual shall be made available to each dive team member.

B. This Manual, NAO 209-123 and all Safety Bulletins can be viewed and downloaded from the NOAA Dive Center (NDC) website at www.ndc.noaa.gov.

C. Each NOAA diver, who is either NOAA-trained or granted equivalency by the NDPM, shall have access to a copy of this document and the NOAA Diving Manual.

1.2   Program Mission, Goals, Core Products, and Services and Management

1.2.1   Program Mission. The mission of the NDP is to "train, certify, and equip scientists, engineers and technicians to perform a variety of underwater tasks in support of NOAA's mission and to ensure that all NOAA diving operations are conducted safely, efficiently and economically, with safety being the primary focus."

1.2.2   Goals, Core Products and Services of the NDP.
   A. Establish standards and implement policies and procedures for conducting safe NOAA diving operations.
   B. Train and certify scientists, engineers, and technicians in diving and diving medicine-related subjects.
   C. Provide NOAA divers with safe, state-of-the-art, and well maintained dive equipment.
   D. Provide guidance and expertise to the NOAA diving community.
   E. Investigate and implement new diving technologies and techniques for NOAA divers.
   F. Provide equipment, personnel and expertise to NOAA field operations, as needed.
   G. Promote NOAA and the NDP through education and outreach.
   H. Promote, facilitate, and implement coordination and communication between private sector, academic and government diving entities.

1.2.3   Management.
   A. The OMAO Director has overall administrative responsibility for the NDP.
   B. Management of the diving program is delegated from the OMAO Director to the NDPM.
   C. The NDCSB reviews and establishes diving regulations, policies, and procedures deemed necessary to ensure a safe and efficient diving program.
   D. As required by 29 CFR 1910, Subpart T, the NDCSB has absolute and autonomous authority over diving operations.

SECTION 2: PERSONNEL

Duties and responsibilities delegated herein to specific roles and positions may not be further re-delegated unless specifically authorized in this Manual.

2.1   Director, Office of Marine and Aviation Operations

2.1.1   General.
   A. The OMAO Director broadly administers NOAA's diving activities.
   B. Responsibility for the day-to-day management of the NDP has been delegated to the NDPM.

2.1.2   Responsibilities.
   A. Overall responsibility for the NDP.
   B. Reviews appeals from NOAA divers terminated from diving by the NDCSB.
   C. Reviews issues raised by members of the NDCSB with dissenting opinions.
   D. Reviews minutes from NDCSB meetings and provides guidance on issues raised by the Board.
   E. Approves candidates for the membership on the NOAA Diving Medical Review Board.
   F. Makes final selection for NDPM position.

2.2   NOAA Diving Program Manager

2.2.1   General.
   A. Selected by the OMAO Director from a certified list of candidates from the Workforce Management Office (WFMO) with recommendations from the NDCSB.
   B. Administers and manages the NDP.
   C. Serves as a voting member of the NDCSB.
   D. May permit aspects of the NDP to be carried out by a qualified designee, although the NDPM may not delegate responsibility for the overall safe conduct of the NDP.

2.2.2   Responsibilities.
   A. Implements all policies and decisions prescribed by the NDCSB;
   B. Responsible to the OMAO Director for the management of the NDP;
   C. Reviews recommendations from the NOAA Diving Safety Officer (NDSO) and takes appropriate action.
   D. Suspends diving operations considered to be unsafe or unwise.
   E. Investigates and reviews new diving technologies and techniques.
   F. Suspends or revokes diving privileges for violating the standards and procedures in this Manual as directed by the NDCSB.

2.2.3   Management and Administration.
   A. Conducts an annual review of all NOAA diving operations and submits a report to OMAO Director.
   B. Monitors and enforces compliance with the applicable federal regulations and the NOAA Diving Standards and Safety Manuals (NDSSM).

2.2.4 Training and Certification.
   A. Determines completion of certification requirements and issues NOAA diver certifications and authorizations to dive.
   B. Signs all "Letters of Authorization to Dive," "Dive Certifications," "Diver ID Cards," and "Letters of Reciprocity" (LOR).

2.2.5 Qualifications.
   A. NOAA certified diver, or equivalent, as determined by the NDCSB.
   B. Have a minimum of 15 years experience in diving or related field.
   C. Broad technical and/or scientific expertise in research related diving (e.g., safety, regulations, equipment, procedures).

2.3   NOAA Diving Control and Safety Board

2.3.1 General.
   A. The NDCSB is an appointed board of representatives from NOAA's Line and Staff Offices (LO/SO) who report to the OMAO Director, and are responsible for the safety and effectiveness of the NDP.
   B. Although the NDCSB reports to the OMAO Director, per 29 CFR 1910, Subpart T, the NDCSB exercises autonomous and absolute authority over operations of the NDP for both working and scientific dives.
   C. The NDCSB shall meet annually in person and should meet monthly via teleconference, unless special meetings are required to address time sensitive issues.

2.3.2 Composition and Qualifications.
   A. The voting members of the NDCSB shall include the following individuals:
      1) NDPM;
      2) LODOs/SODO with active diving programs;
      3) NOAA Deputy Line and Staff Office Diving Officers (DLODOs/DSODO) with active diving programs; and
      4) NDSO.
   B. The NOAA Diving Program Diving Medical Officer (NDP DMO) shall be a non-voting member of the NDCSB.
   C. The NDCSB may consult individual advisors or advisory panels with subject matter expertise to provide additional information.
   D. All Members of the NDCSB shall be NOAA certified divers with a majority being qualified, active scientific divers.
   E. A separate, non-voting Executive Secretariat, appointed by the Chairperson, may be appointed to assist the NDCSB administratively.

2.3.3 Selection of NDCSB Members.
   A. NDPM is selected by the OMAO Director from a list of candidates provided by the WFMO.
   B. LODOs are appointed by NOAA Assistant Administrators from LOs with active diving programs.
   C. SODO is appointed by the OMAO Director.
   D. DLODOs/DSODOs are appointed by the respective LODO/SODO with concurrence of their immediate supervisors.

2.3.4 Chairperson.
    A. The Chairperson shall be selected from the remaining list of voting members by majority vote of all voting members.
    B. To avoid conflict of responsibilities, the NDSO is not eligible to serve as the Board Chairperson.

2.3.5 Decision Making Process.
    A. The Chairperson shall strive for consensus on all NDCSB issues and decisions, and every attempt shall be made to query each voting member of the NDCSB on all decisions.
    B. A quorum of two-thirds of the voting members must be present, in person or electronically, to conduct official business.
    C. Decisions will be made by majority vote with the Chairperson casting the deciding vote in case of a tie.
    D. Major objections to majority votes shall be made part of the meeting minutes. Any voting member of the NDCSB may request that an item be raised to the OMAO Director via written communication from the Chairperson.

2.3.6 Term Limits.
    A. The Chairperson shall serve a 1 year term, and may be re-elected.
    B. The NDPM and NDSO are non-rotating members of the NDCSB. All other members should serve a maximum of 5 consecutive years.
    C. Appointments should be scheduled so only one (1) member rotates off the NDCSB per year.

2.3.7 Responsibilities.
    A. General.
        1) Exercises autonomous and absolute authority over and promotes the safe and effective operations of the NDP for both working and scientific dives;
        2) Establishes such processes and program structure as necessary to effectively approve and monitor diving projects across NOAA's geographically dispersed diving program;
        3) Reviews and approves all working diving operations involving equipment other than open-circuit SCUBA, breathing mixtures other than air, or depths greater than 100 fsw; Reviews and approves all scientific diving operations involving equipment other than open-circuit SCUBA, breathing mixtures other than air or Nitrox, depths greater than 130 fsw or bottom times beyond the U.S. Navy no-decompression limits; and
        4) Delegates authority to Unit Diving Supervisors (UDS) to review and approve routine dive operations conducted at the unit level.
    B. Safety.
        1) Ensures sufficient oversight for safety exists within NDP;
        2) Participates in safety assessments as necessary;
        3) Advises the OMAO Director, and the Safety and Environmental Compliance Office (SECO) Director of circumstances adversely impacting safety and/or efficiency of the NDP; and
        4) Instructs and reminds divers, LDs, DMs, and UDSs to adhere to all NDP diving regulations, standards, policies, and procedures.

C. Incident Review and Action.
   1) Serves as a board of review for inquiries into the nature and cause of diving incidents (including near-misses) as well as violations of NOAA or other applicable policies and standards, and reports the results to the OMAO Director and the SECO Director;
   2) For Class 'A' incidents involving a fatality or severe injury, or other cases constituting a "serious incident" under the NOAA Safety Policy (NAO 209-1), responsibility for the conduct of the official investigation and corrective action is retained by SECO (Appendix 14);
   3) Institutes appropriate measures to mitigate the reoccurrence of dive incidents; and
   4) Prescribes action for unsafe or noncompliant practices or actions.
D. Manuals and Procedures.
   1) Develops and promulgates standards and safety manuals, and reviews and revises them as necessary;
   2) Monitors compliance with standards and safety manuals, including establishing such compliance inspection and certification programs as necessary, and reports non-compliance to the NDPM for action; and
   3) Reviews and makes changes in other NOAA diving regulations, standards, policies, and operational procedures.
E. Training and Certification.
   1) Establishes and/or approves training and certification programs for NOAA divers and non-NOAA divers participating in NOAA-sponsored dive projects;
   2) Reviews, adopts, and enforces physical conditioning and medical standards required to promote diver safety;
   3) Recommends to the NDPM the revocation of diving certifications;
   4) Determines equivalency of applicant entities with that of the NDP for diving reciprocity; and
   5) Considers appeals from divers whose dive certifications are suspended.
F. Standardized Equipment Program.
   1) Considers, reviews, and makes appropriate changes in diving equipment requirements; and
   2) Reviews and approves new diving technologies and techniques for possible implementation.

2.4   NOAA Diving Safety Officer

2.4.1   General.
A. The NDSO is selected by the OMAO Director from a certified list of candidates from WFMO with recommendation from the NDCSB.
B. Reports to the OMAO Director.
C. Voting member of the NDCSB.

2.4.2   Responsibilities.
A. Provides advice to the NDCSB, NOAA managers, and divers for working and scientific diving safety and health related issues.
B. Provides assistance with NOAA diving safety issues to other NOAA offices and coordinates resolution of NOAA diving safety issues as directed by the OMAO Director.

C. Coordinates annual safety inspections of all NOAA dive units and provides findings to the NDPM, NDCSB, and OMAO Director.

D. May permit portions of this program to be carried out by a qualified delegate, although the NDSO may not delegate responsibility for the overall safe conduct of the NDP.

E. Investigates, subject to and consistent with the incident investigation parameters in NAO 209-1, all Class B diving mishaps and provides findings to the NDPM, NDCSB, OMAO Director, and SECO Director (Appendix 14).

F. Suspends diving operations considered to be unsafe or unwise and reports this action to the NDCSB. Reauthorization for diving may be granted by the LODO/SODO after the completion of a Corrective Action Plan (CAP).

G. As directed by the OMAO Director, assesses appropriateness and consistency of diving safety requirements for NOAA federal, grant, and contract procedures, and provides recommendations to appropriate NOAA managers and the NDCSB.

H. Conducts an annual safety assessment of the NDP and such other ad hoc assessments as appropriate or as directed by the OMAO Director, and reports on the results of such assessments to the OMAO Director and the NDCSB including recommendations or actions taken to strengthen the safety and effectiveness of the NDP.

2.4.3 Qualifications.
A. NOAA DM or equivalent as determined by the NDCSB;
B. Have a minimum of 10 years experience in diving;
C. Broad technical and/or scientific expertise in research related diving (e.g., safety, regulations, equipment, procedures); and
D. Shall be a current or previously-certified SCUBA instructor from an internationally recognized certifying agency.

2.5 Line and Staff Office Diving Officers

2.5.1 General.
A. Senior representatives for diving for each of the NOAA Line (NOS, NMFS, OAR) and Staff (OMAO) Offices.
B. LODOs are appointed by their respective Assistant Administrators, with concurrence of the NDCSB and approval of the employee's immediate supervisor.
C. The SODO is appointed by the OMAO Director, with concurrence of the NDCSB and approval of the employee's immediate supervisor.
D. Duties and responsibilities are included in the LODO/SODO performance plans.

2.5.2 Responsibilities.
A. Safety.
1) Conducts, or delegates, annual on-site diving unit safety inspections, and forwards reports to the NDSO by January 31 of each year.
2) Serves as subject matter experts, as requested, for the SECO and the SECO-assigned investigative teams for incidents involving a fatality or severe injury, or other criteria constituting a "serious incident" under the NOAA Safety Policy (NAO 209-1). Note: Responsibility for conducting the investigation and tracking completion of corrective actions is retained by SECO.

3) Reviews diving accidents and incidents which are not covered in the previous item that occur within the respective Line/Staff Offices (LO/SO), and reports findings, recommendations, and/or proposed changes to the NDSO.

4) Suspends divers and/or diving operations considered to be unsafe or unwise.

5) Assists in administration of Diving Unit Safety Assessment (DUSA) program.

B. Management and Administration.

1) Assists as needed in planning and reviewing advanced and/or remote diving operations of assigned units and ensures compliance with this Manual.

2) Maintains familiarity with diving activities within assigned units and submits annual report to the NDPM by November 31 of each year for the preceding fiscal year.

C. Training. Determines recertification requirements for divers whose diving authorizations have lapsed by more than 6 months, per Section 3.5.

D. SEP. Verifies accuracy of annual SEP assessment charges for assigned units.

2.5.3 Qualifications.

A. Be a current or former NOAA certified Advanced Working diver.

B. Meet the requirements for UDS in Section 2.6.

C. Have a minimum of 10 years experience in diving.

D. Must be current in cardiopulmonary resuscitation (CPR), including adult Automated External Defibrillator (AED), first aid and oxygen administration and be knowledgeable in dive accident management.

2.6   Deputy Line and Staff Office Diving Officers

2.6.1 General.

A. DLODO/DSODO are representatives for diving for each of the NOAA Line (NOS, NMFS, OAR) and Staff (OMAO) Offices.

B. DLODOs are appointed by their LODOs with approval of the employee's immediate supervisor.

C. The DSODO is appointed by the SODO with approval of the employee's immediate supervisor.

D. Duties and responsibilities are included in the DLODO/DSODO performance plans.

E. Term of service is 1 year, but may be extended by the respective LODO/SODO.

2.6.2 Responsibilities.

A. Serves as a voting member of the NDCSB.

B. Assists LODOs/SODO in the performance of assigned duties as requested.

2.6.3 Qualifications.

A. Be a current or former NOAA certified Advanced Working diver.

B. Meet the requirements for UDS in Section 2.6.

C. Have a minimum of 7 years experience in diving.

2.7   Unit Diving Supervisors

2.7.1 General.

A. Assigned throughout the agency to provide administrative oversight of divers at the facility level within their respective LO/SO.
B. Assigned by their LODO/SODO with concurrence of the NDCSB and approval of the employee's immediate supervisor.
C. Duties and responsibilities are included in UDS's performance plans and may be delegated as appropriate.

2.7.2   Responsibilities.
A.   Safety.
   1) Ensures all diving is planned and conducted in accordance with all prescribed NOAA diving standards, policies, and procedures listed in this Manual, as well as meets the requirements for the scientific exemption outlined in OSHA 29 CFR 1910, Subpart T;
   2) Ensures competent DMs or LDs are in charge of operations at dive sites;
   3) Ensures all diving gear and accessory equipment is maintained in a safe operating condition;
   4) Reports all diving-related accidents/incidents that occur within their units to their LODO/SODO as prescribed in this Manual, and consistent with NAO 209-1;
   5) Approves dive plans and Diving Emergency Assistance Plans (DEAP) for all routine dives involving no-decompression profiles, open circuit SCUBA and using air or Nitrox as a breathing gas;
   6) Elevates to the NDCSB all non-routine dive plans and emergency assistance plans for approval prior to commencement of the diving operation;
   7) Suspends divers and/or dive operations when deemed necessary and notifies the NDC and their respective LODO/SODO within 48 hours;
   8) Conducts a check out dive(s) with all recently certified divers or those transferring from another unit to familiarize them with local conditions, protocols, procedures, and unique hazards prior to permitting unrestricted operational diving;
   9) Ensures that any diving conducted using specialized equipment or procedures (e.g., drysuits, full face masks, tethered or line-tended SCUBA) is practiced on an annual basis to maintain diver proficiency. Failure to meet these minimum standards requires work-up (refresher) dives to be conducted prior to making operational dives; and
   10) Ensures semi-annual air purity tests are completed on all NOAA-owned air compressors and takes corrective action if results are out-of-specifications as delegated by the UDS.
   11) Assists in administration of DUSA program.
B.   Management and Administration.
   1) Disseminates NOAA diving standards, policies, and procedures to assigned divers;
   2) Maintains or delegates to qualified personnel the responsibility of record keeping (e.g., Letters of Certification, training, and equipment) for assigned divers;
   4) Ensures all divers are certified, properly trained, and fit to perform the required diving;
   5) Conducts or delegates annual dive locker inspection and submits report to their respective LODO/SODO by January 15 of each year;
   6) Submits report of unit diving activities for the preceding fiscal year to their respective LODO/SODO by November 15 of each year;
   7) Prepares diver training applications and submits them to NDC; and

8) Forwards a copy of all approved dive plans and Diving Emergency Assistance Plans (DEAP) to the appropriate DM or LD responsible for the dive operation and to ndp.diveplans@noaa.gov.

C. Training. Conducts operational training and conducts skills evaluation check-out dives as needed.

D. Standardized Equipment Program.
1) Keeps NDC apprised of changes to unit roster;
2) Tracks SEP equipment and ensures gear is returned to NDC upon departure of divers from unit;
3) Verifies accuracy of annual SEP assessment charges for assigned divers; and
4) Helps facilitate collection of fees by ensuring a local budget office has the accounting codes from divers' supervisors.

2.7.3 Qualifications.
A. Be a current or former NOAA certified diver;
B. Complete the NOAA DM training program;
C. Should have a minimum of 5 years experience in diving;
D. Demonstrates ability to conduct operational training and skills evaluation checkout dives; and
E. Must be current in CPR, including adult AED, first aid and oxygen administration, and be knowledgeable in dive accident management.

2.8 Divemasters and Lead Divers

2.8.1 General.
A. DMs and LDs shall be in charge of all aspects of the diving operation at the dive site and shall:
1) Have the experience and training in the conduct of the assigned diving operation;
2) Have authority over execution of on-site diving operations; and
3) Be at the dive location.
B. DMs and LDs may dive as long as there is a qualified topside person, designated by the DM or LD, to render assistance in an emergency.
C. Duties and responsibilities are included in DM's performance plans.

2.8.2 Responsibilities.
A. Safety.
1) Ensures all diving is planned and conducted in accordance with all prescribed NOAA diving standards, policies, and procedures listed in this Manual, as well as all applicable OSHA standards outlined in 29 CFR 1910, Subpart T;
2) Submits dive plans to UDS for approval;
3) Prohibits any diver from diving who, in their opinion, exhibits problems of a physical or psychological nature that may compromise the safety of a diver or the dive team;
4) Suspends diving operations when unusual hazards or environmental conditions adversely affect the safety of the diving operation;
5) Ensures emergency procedures are established and clearly understood by all personnel before diving begins;
6) Ensures all safety and emergency equipment is in working order and at the dive site;

7) Ensures all divers are monitored after each dive for signs or symptoms of decompression sickness or other diving-related maladies;

8) Reports all diving-related accidents and incidents as prescribed in this Manual and NAO 209-1;

9) Coordinates with other known activities in the vicinity that are likely to interfere with diving operations;

10) Ensures all diver-worn equipment is properly configured in accordance with the standards outlined in this Manual;

11) Obtains concurrence from the vessel captain and ensures all vessel pre-dive checklists (e.g., NOAA Form 64-3) have been completed prior to initiating diving operations when applicable;

12) Conducts pre- and post-dive safety briefings; and

13) Assists in administration of DUSA program.

B. Management and Administration.

1) Ensures files are maintained if delegated by the UDS; and

2) Ensures qualified individuals are assigned to fulfill all required diving and support positions.

C. Training. Conducts operational training and skills evaluation check-out dives of divers as directed by the UDS.

D. Standardized Equipment Program.

1) Ensures all equipment is in safe operating condition, and required maintenance records are maintained if delegated by their UDS; and

2) Assists UDS in tracking SEP equipment and ensures gear is returned to NDC upon departure of divers from unit.

2.8.3 Qualifications.

A. Divemaster.

1) Be a current or former NOAA certified diver unless authorized by the LODO/SODO;

2) Complete the NOAA DM training program;

3) Be assigned by the UDS; and

4) Must be current in CPR, including adult AED, first aid and oxygen administration and be knowledgeable in dive accident management.

B. Lead Diver.

1) Be a current NOAA certified diver;

2) Be approved by the UDS or designee after demonstrating the ability to properly plan and safely execute dive operations; and

3) Must be current in CPR, including adult AED, first aid and oxygen administration, and be knowledgeable in dive accident management.

2.9   Ship Diving Officer

2.9.1 General.

A. A ship Diving Officer is a designated crewmember of a NOAA ship who serves as the primary communicator between NDP and the ship.

B. Ensures NDP and ship's Command understand each other's needs and requirements.

C. Does not plan or supervise dive operations unless currently certified as a DM by the NDP.

    D. Reports to an assigned OMAO UDS in the diving chain of command.

2.9.2 Responsibilities.
    A. Administers NDP policies onboard specific OMAO ship as delegated by the assigned shore-based UDS.
    B. Monitors dive roster and informs Command of issues affecting operational readiness, (e.g., such as lapsing proficiency, expiring certification, training requirements, and personnel shortages).
    C. Prepares, or delegates to the diver candidate, diver training applications and submits them to NDC.
    D. Maintains the ship's dive operations manual and other NDP-required documents, including personnel training records, air compressor maintenance records, and this Manual.
    E. Conducts semi-annual air compressor testing in accordance with the NDP TRI Air Testing Program.
    F. Submits report of unit diving activities for the preceding fiscal year to the SODO by November 15 of each year.
    G. Conducts an annual dive locker inspection and submits report to their respective UDS by January 15 of each year.
    H. Assists in administration of DUSA program.

2.9.3 Qualifications.
    A. May be any crewmember duly appointed by the Commanding Officer.
    B. Must have good organizational and communication skills.
    C. Should receive and give thorough instructions when rotating and/or reassigning shipboard duties.

2.10 Scientific Divers

2.10.1 General.
    A. Divers are assigned throughout the agency to conduct underwater tasks in support of NOAA's scientific mission.
    B. NOAA divers shall be certified to dive by the NDP and be sufficiently trained and experienced to undertake assigned diving tasks safely and effectively.

2.10.2 Responsibilities.
    A. Adheres to the standards contained within this Manual when conducting scientific dives.
    B. Refuses to dive when in their judgment, conditions are unsafe, or if they would be violating the precepts of their training or the requirements in this Manual.
    C. Maintains good physical condition and a high level of diving proficiency.
    D. Reports to the DM or LD any changes of a physical or psychological nature that may adversely impact their or their buddy's fitness to dive.
    E. Will not begin or continue a dive if problems exist of a physical or psychological nature that can compromise the safety of the diver or dive team.
    F. Ensures diving equipment used is maintained in a safe operating condition.
    G. Is accountable for NOAA-issued equipment.

H. Adheres to the buddy system, actively monitors buddy status, including, but not limited to, cylinder pressure, and intervenes to the maximum extent practicable to ensure the safety of the dive team.

I. Refrain from the use of illegal drugs that could compromise the safety of the diver or dive team.

J. Assists in administration of DUSA program.

2.10.3 Qualifications. NOAA divers shall meet the requirements outlined in Section 3.1 of this Manual.

2.11 Temporary Scientific Divers

2.11.1 General.
A. Occasionally there may be situations where highly qualified, non-NOAA divers could significantly contribute to a dive project, but:
1) Are not currently certified as a NOAA Scientific Diver; or
2) Due to the limited extent of the project, full NOAA diver certification would not be reasonable or appropriate.
B. Temporary Scientific Divers are eligible to participate in NOAA-sponsored dive operations for a specific project or limited period of time.
C. The NDCSB will ultimately determine:
1) Which candidates meet the requirements for Temporary Scientific Diver certification; and
2) Any limitations imposed on the divers.
D. Temporary Scientific Divers diving under NOAA auspices shall follow the standards outlined in this Manual.

2.11.2 Medical Requirements. Candidates must successfully complete a medical examination in accordance with the standards outlined in the NOAA Diving Medical Standards and Procedures Manual.

2.11.3 Minimum Requirements.
A. Proof of training and/or experience equivalent to that of a NOAA Scientific Diver as determined by the NDCSB.
B. Current certification in CPR, including adult AED, first aid, and oxygen administration (American Heart Association, American Red Cross, or equivalent).
C. Successful completion of NOAA Scientific Diver exam.
D. Successful completion of a swim test and open-water checkout dive equivalent to that required for NOAA divers.
E. Successful completion of the NOAA Diving Regulations, Policies, and Procedures lesson found on the NDC website at www.ndc.noaa.gov
F. A minimum of 25 logged dives.
G. Successful completion of applicable NOAA specialized training (e.g., DUI Weight and Trim System, Gas Consumption Calculation, RASS, Line-tended Standby Diver) as deemed appropriate by the NDCSB.
H. Approval of the NDCSB.

2.11.4 Limitations.
  A. Temporary Scientific Diver certifications are valid for up to 6 months as determined by the NDCSB and may be extended for one (1) additional 6 month period.
  B. Maximum depth and tasks authorized will be based on review of the divers' resumes and dive logs.

2.11.5 Equipment. With LODO/SODO and work supervisor's approval, Temporary Scientific Divers may be outfitted with SEP equipment per Section 5.3.1.

2.12 Observer Divers

2.12.1 General.
  A. NOAA program sites are frequently visited by representatives of other agencies, the media, and various officials for the purpose of familiarization, evaluation, or reporting on NOAA programs.
  B. The NOAA Observer Diver classification was established to allow divers to observe diving activities conducted by NOAA.
  C. Observer Divers diving under NOAA auspices on scientific dives shall follow the standards outlined in this Manual.
  D. Once authorized, participation of Observer Divers shall be solely at the discretion of the DM or LD.

2.12.2 Eligibility.
  A. The Observer Diver classification is open to both NOAA and non-NOAA personnel.
  B. This classification does not apply to NOAA employees who dive as part of their regular duties or to NOAA employees who have been determined to be medically unqualified to dive.

2.12.3 Minimum Requirements.
  A. Persons seeking authority to participate as an Observer Diver must provide the following documents to the appropriate UDS:
    1) Evidence of diving certification from a recognized diver certifying organization (e.g., National Association of Underwater Instructors (NAUI), Professional Association of Diving Instructors (PADI), or the military);
    3) Evidence of 10 logged dives, one of which has been conducted within the previous 3 months, indicating the appropriate proficiencies required for the diving conditions likely to be encountered; and
    4) Applicants must:
      a) Complete the NDP Observer Diver Medical History Report form and submit it directly to the NDP DMO for evaluation and approval; and if non-NOAA
      b) Sign the Assumption of Risk and Release of Liability for Guests and Observer Divers Diving with the National Oceanic and Atmospheric Administration (NOAA) form.
  B. The NOAA UDS or designee shall:
    1) Inspect diver's credentials and determine whether they have presented evidence establishing certifications by approved organizations;
    2) Use NOAA Form 56-62, NOAA Observer Diver Report, to obtain a signed liability release from the diver (non-NOAA employees only) and complete the checklist portion (all Observer divers);

3) Inspect diver's gear for proper operating condition and require replacement of items not considered serviceable;

4) Review diver's equipment maintenance records and verify the equipment has been serviced within the previous 12 months;

5) Obtain approval from the LODO/SODO;

6) Upon receiving clearance, conduct in-water evaluations of observer candidates to determine if current and overall experience levels, fitness, and diving proficiencies are adequate for the conditions likely to be encountered on the dives; and

7) Complete the dive log section of NOAA Form 56-62, NOAA Observer Diver Report, immediately following the diving operation and forward to the NDC.

C. The LODO/SODO shall:

1) Receive a request from the UDS;

2) Receive medical clearance from NDP DMO;

3) Make the final decision on whether to authorize; and

4) Inform the UDS of the decision.

2.12.4 Limitations.

A. Tasks of Observer Divers are limited to observation, photography and/or videography.

B. Observer Divers may participate in up to six (6) dives a year unless authorized by the LODO/SODO.

2.12.5 Manning Requirements.

A. Escort Divers.

1) Observer Divers must be accompanied by a minimum of 2 UDS-approved authorized NOAA divers whose sole responsibilities are to monitor the observer in order to ensure his/her safety.

2) A buddy team of NOAA escort divers may accompany up to 2 observer divers.

3) Additional observer divers require additional NOAA escort divers in a ratio of one to one (See table below).

B. Standby Divers. A team of standby divers, or a line-tended standby diver, shall be available topside and ready to enter the water within 1 minute of notification unless waived by the LODO/SODO.

C. A Designated Person In-Charge who is assigned by the DM or LD and stationed topside at the dive location, shall be in charge of all aspects of the dive operation affecting the safety and health of the dive team members.

Observer Divers	Escort Divers	Standby Divers[1]	DPIC
1	2	1 or 2	1
2	2	1 or 2	1
3	3	1 or 2	1
4	4	1 or 2	1

Note [1]: See Section 2.11.5 B above.

2.12.6 Equipment.

A. Unless authorized by the LODO/SODO, Observer Divers shall be outfitted with personally-supplied diving equipment equivalent to that of Section 5.3.1.

B. Each escort diver shall carry a RASS.

2.13 Reciprocity Scientific Diver

2.13.1 General.
  A. Non-NOAA divers may participate in NOAA diving activities, and NOAA divers may participate in non-NOAA diving activities through reciprocity agreements.
  B. Scientific reciprocity divers under NOAA auspices shall follow the standards outlined in this Manual.
  C. NOAA reciprocity agreements:
    1) Allow non-NOAA divers to participate in NOAA diving activities, and vice-versa with minimal administrative requirements;
    2) Are established with other organizations only after it is determined that their diving programs are equivalent to NOAA's;
    3) Are only applicable to personnel employed and covered for medical treatment and Workers Compensation by reciprocity organizations;
    4) Are not transferable to other agencies or institutions with whom NOAA's reciprocity partners have separate reciprocity agreements with; and
    5) Expire on December 31 of the year in which they were established. They must be re-established annually.
  D. Reciprocity divers in good standing with their organizations, who are not employees (e.g., students) and are not covered for medical treatment and Workers Compensation, can only be accepted as volunteers if permitted by statutory authority (Section 2.13).

2.13.2 Request for Reciprocity with a Non-NOAA Organization.
  A. A NOAA UDS may request formal diving reciprocity be established with non-NOAA organizations when no such agreement exists.
  B. Such requests, along with a copy of the candidate organization's diving standards and safety manual, must be forwarded through the appropriate LODO/SODO to the NDCSB for review.
  C. If deemed equivalent to NOAA's diving standards, reciprocity may be established for the current calendar year.
  D. Reciprocity agreements are reviewed at the end of the calendar year and may be renewed at the request of the sponsoring UDS.
  E. A list of current reciprocity agreements is maintained on the website at www.ndc.noaa.gov.

2.13.3 Letters of Reciprocity for NOAA Divers.
  A. Per the terms of the reciprocity agreements, any NOAA diver wanting to dive with a reciprocity organization must request a LOR be sent from the NDPM to the DSO of the receiving organization verifying they are an authorized NOAA Diver. In exigent circumstances, the UDS may issue a LOR but must notify the NDPM within 24 hours.
  B. The NDP Letter of Reciprocity Request Form, available on the NDC website, must be completed and sent to the NDC for processing.
  C. LORs are generated by the NDC, signed by the NDPM, and forwarded to the receiving DSO with a copy to the NOAA diver.
  D. LORs will only be sent if the NOAA diver is in an authorized diving status requiring the following:
    1) Dive proficiency (a minimum of 3 dives per quarter);
    2) Approved dive physical (per age-based requirements); and

      3) Medical Training (CPR, including adult AED, first aid, and oxygen administration).

E. Liability information.

     1) LORs for NOAA federal full-time employees will state the diver is covered under the Federal Employee Compensation Act, United States Code (USC) 5 USC § 8101 *et seq.*, for injuries that may be sustained as the result of an accident occurring during the scope of any official dive; as well as by the provisions of the Federal Tort Claims Act, 28 USC §§ 1346, 2671 *et seq.*; and

     2) LORs for NOAA contract employees will state the diver is not a federal employee and, therefore, not covered by NOAA for injuries that may be sustained as the result of an accident occurring during the scope of any official dive.

F. LORs only address a diver's credentials and status within the NDP; it is up to the LO Program Office to which the diver belongs to determine if the specific work to be performed with a reciprocity partner is authorized from a programmatic standpoint.

2.13.4 Letters of Reciprocity for Non-NOAA Divers.

A. Reciprocity divers wanting to dive with NOAA must present a signed LOR from their organization's DSO to the appropriate UDS, or designee verifying that the diver is in an authorized status with their organization.

B. Must indicate the diver is covered for medical treatment and covered under their organization's Workers Compensation policy.

C. Must be received from the DSO at an institution with whom NOAA currently has reciprocity.

D. Must meet the NOAA diving proficiency requirements (i.e., three (3) dives during previous quarter).

2.13.5 Equipment.

A. Reciprocity Scientific Divers shall be outfitted with personally-supplied diving equipment equivalent to that of Section 5.3.1 as determined by the on-site DM or LD.

B. A UDS will inspect the Reciprocity Diver's non-NOAA diving equipment for proper operating condition and replace items not considered serviceable with other equipment provided by the diver or NOAA.

C. When not provided by the Reciprocity Diver and with verification of the appropriate training, NOAA shall provide (when required) a diver-carried reserve breathing gas supply to the diver.

2.14   Volunteer Scientific Divers

2.14.1 General.

A. The Federal Government may only accept voluntary services as provided for by statute. Two laws that allow NOAA to accept volunteer services for certain activities are the Fish and Wildlife Improvement Act of 1978, 16 USC 742f, and the National Marine Sanctuary Act, 16 USC 1442.

B. The Fish and Wildlife Improvement Act authorizes Secretaries of the Interior and Commerce (inclusive of NOAA) to recruit, train, and accept the services of volunteer workers for or in aid of programs related to fish and wildlife programs or activities. The Act also authorizes provision of incidental expenses such as transportation, lodging, awards, and subsistence to volunteers without regard to their place of residence.

C. The National Marine Sanctuaries Act states that NOAA may accept donations of funds, property, and services for use in designating and administering National Marine Sanctuaries.

D. NOAA Volunteer Divers conducting approved diving work authorized by the Fish and Wildlife Act, as amended, or the National Marine Sanctuaries Act, as amended, or other applicable statutes will in most circumstances be considered federal employees for purposes of claims under the Federal Tort Claims Act and for purposes of the Federal Employees' Compensation Act.

E. Volunteers must submit proof of training and experience to the appropriate NOAA UDS for review. The UDS will forward documentation, along with his/her recommendation, to their LODO/SODO. The LODO/SODO will forward documentation, along with his/her recommendation, to the NDPM. The NDPM will review the documentation and recommendations from the UDS and LODO/SODO and render a decision. The NDPM will notify the LODO/SODO and UDS of his/her decision.

2.14.2 Eligibility.

A. NOAA Volunteer Scientific Divers must be sponsored by a NOAA program or office. An appointing officer from that program or office is responsible for meeting all federal requirements for administering and managing the work of the volunteer and serves as the point of contact to the NDPM.

B. Divers in good standing with organizations with whom NOAA has an active Reciprocity Agreement for diving, and who meet the requirements of Section 2.13.4 may be accepted as volunteers based on their diving credentials as reciprocity divers.

C. Individuals not meeting the above requirement must comply with all diving regulations, policies, and procedures prescribed in this Manual for NOAA certified divers.

2.14.3 Authority for Accepting Volunteers.

A. Authority for accepting volunteers for liability rests with the specific NOAA office/program hiring official receiving the services of the volunteer.

B. Final authority for certifying volunteers as NOAA divers rests with the NDPM.

2.14.4 Minimum Requirements.

A. Successful completion of a medical examination equivalent to those standards outlined in this NOAA Diving Medical Standards and Procedures Manual.

B. Proof of training and/or experience equivalent to that of a NOAA Diver as determined by the NDCSB and verified by the UDS. A minimum of 30 logged dives is required.

C. Current CPR, including adult AED, first aid, and oxygen administration certifications (American Heart Association, American Red Cross, or equivalent) and verified by the UDS.

D. Successful completion of a written test of knowledge as determined by the NDCSB and verified by the UDS or designee.

E. Successful completion of the NOAA swim test (Section 3.1.4) and an open-water checkout dive equivalent to that required for NOAA Divers and conducted by the UDS, or designee.

F. Successful completion of applicable NOAA specialized training (e.g., DUI Weight and Trim System, Gas consumption calculation, RASS, Line-tended Standby Diver) verified by UDS.

G. Submit to voluntary drug testing (Section 3.1.3).

H. Approval of the NDPM.

2.14.5 Limitations.

A. Maximum depth and tasks authorized may be limited by the UDS, LODO/SODO, or the NDPM based on review of the diver's resume and dive logs.

B. Unless approved by the UDS, Volunteer Scientific Divers shall be directly supervised by an on-site NOAA DM or LD. If a DM or LD is not available, the UDS may assign supervisory responsibility to another NOAA employee, but only if the individual is knowledgeable in the diving activities being conducted and is ready, willing, and able to render assistance in an emergency.

C. Must be at least 18 years of age.

2.14.6 Equipment.

A. Unless authorized by the UDS, Volunteer Scientific Divers shall be outfitted with their own diving equipment equivalent to that of NOAA divers, and annual service records will be provided to the UDS for review. The responsibility for any lost or damaged volunteer-owned diving gear or equipment rests with the sponsoring program or office.

B. When not provided by the Volunteer Diver, and with verification of appropriate training, NOAA shall provide (when required) the diver with a diver-carried RASS to be used while performing official NOAA dives.

2.14.7 Responsibilities.

A. NOAA Appointing Officer.

1) Reviews and approves all requests for Volunteer Scientific Divers from a NOAA office/program perspective.

2) Signs all required volunteer forms acknowledging approval and acceptance of liability for the volunteer while providing volunteer service to the NOAA office/program.

B. Volunteer Diver.

1) Adheres to the standards contained within this Manual when conducting scientific dives.

2) Refuses to dive when in their judgment, conditions are unsafe, or if they would be violating the precepts of their training or the requirements in this Manual.

3) Maintains good physical condition and a high level of diving proficiency.

4) Reports to the DM or LD any changes of a physical or psychological nature that may adversely impact their or their buddy's fitness to dive.

5) Will not begin or continue a dive if problems exist of a physical or psychological nature that can compromise the safety of the diver or dive team.

6) Ensures diving equipment used is maintained in a safe operating condition.

7) Adheres to the buddy system, actively monitors buddy status, including, but not limited to, cylinder pressure, and intervenes to the maximum extent practicable to ensure the safety of the dive team.

8) Refrains from the use of illegal drugs.

C. NOAA Unit Diving Supervisor.

1) Reviews documentation from the applicant for compliance with minimum requirements.

   2) Inspects Volunteer Scientific Divers' equipment for proper operating condition, reviews maintenance records, and replaces items not considered serviceable with other equipment provided by the diver or with NOAA equipment.
   3) Administers the written examination and conducts or delegates authority to conduct checkout dive(s).
   4) Forwards documentation to LODO/SODO along with recommendation.
   5) Approves individuals to supervise volunteer diving activities.
D. NOAA LODO/SODO. Reviews documentation and recommendations from the UDS, and forwards to the NDPM within 10 business days.
E. NOAA Diving Program Manager.
   1) Reviews documentation and recommendation from the UDS and LODO/SODO and makes final decision on acceptance of candidate.
   2) Reports decision to LODO/SODO and UDS in writing within 10 days of receipt of package from LODO/SODO.

2.15   Special Task Endorsement Divers

2.15.1 General.
A. NOAA scientific divers may apply for a Special Task Endorsement (STE) for one or more specific working diver tasks (e.g., use of lift bags to move >100 lbs. underwater) to UDSs.
B. Such requests must include a rationale/justification for the endorsement, a detailed outline of the training to be conducted including, but not limited to, the number of hours of classroom and practical instruction, location, and number of training dives to be performed; topside and underwater skills to be performed; and the name and credentials of instructors involved in the training.

2.15.2 Responsibilities.
A. NOAA UDS. The UDS will review the request and, if deemed complete and appropriate, forward it with a recommendation to the appropriate LODO/SODO for review and approval.
B. NOAA LODO/SODO. If approved, the LODO/SODO will forward a request to the NOAA NDPM for issuance of the STE.
C. NOAA NDPM. The NDPM will add the endorsement to the diver's letter of authorization to dive and forward a copy of the letter to the diver, UDS, and LODO/SODO.

2.15.3 Limitations.
A. STEs are valid for 12 consecutive months from the date of award and may be renewed at the discretion of the UDS and LODO/SODO. Divers interested in renewing their STE shall submit a request through their UDS to their LODO/SODO listing the number and types of STE dives performed during the previous award period. The UDS will review the request and, if deemed complete and appropriate, forward it with a recommendation to the appropriate LODO/SODO for review and approval.
B. Once awarded, STE divers are expected to perform the specific task(s) for which the STE was granted at least twice a year. Failure to do so may result in the temporary suspension or revocation of the STE as determined by the LODO/SODO, or his designee.

C. Tasks associated with STEs cannot be conducted as scientific dives under the provisions outlined in 29 CFR 1910.401(a)(2)(iv) and, therefore, must be conducted as "working dives" per 29 CFR1910, Subpart T, and the NOAA Working Diving Standards and Safety Manual.

2.16 NOAA Diving Medical Officer

2.16.1 Definition. A NOAA Diving Medical Officer (DMO) is a health care provider with specialized training in diving and hyperbaric medicine capable of recognizing and providing medical services and/or advice for diving related injuries.

2.16.2 Qualifications.
A. Be a licensed health care provider (physician (MD/DO), nurse practitioner (NP), or physician's assistant (PA) assigned to NOAA; and
B. Complete a NOAA-recognized hyperbaric training course approved by the Chairperson NOAA Diving Medical Review Board (NDMRB) (e.g., NOAA/Undersea and Hyperbaric Medical Society (UHMS) Physicians Training in Diving Medicine course, U.S. Navy's Recognition and Treatment of Diving Injuries course).
C. In addition, the DMO stationed at the NDC will hold and maintain a NOAA diving certification.

2.16.3 Responsibilities.
A. Maintains current education in the area of dive medicine.
B. Conducts reviews of dive physicals and other medical submissions.
C. Makes determinations of medical fitness to dive.
D. Serves as an advisor to the NDPM regarding medical issues.
E. Provides medical services and advice in support of diving operations.
F. Provides medical training.
G. Serves as a liaison between the civilian dive medicine community and the NDC.
H. Serves as Chairperson of the NDMRB and advisor on the NDCSB as appointed by the OMAO Director.
I. Confers with NDMRB as needed to resolve fitness to dive and other dive medicine issues.

2.17 NOAA Diving Medical Review Board

2.17.1 General.
A. The NOAA Diving Medical Review Board (NDMRB) is a standing committee of a minimum of 5 qualified hyperbaric physicians that advises the NDP on various diving-related medical issues.
B. Members of the NDMRB are appointed by the OMAO Director after consultation with the NDPM and the Chair, NDMRB.
C. The NDP DMO shall serve as the Chair, NDMRB.
D. Appointments to the NDMRB are for a period of 5 years and may be extended by the OMAO Director after consultation with the NDPM, and the Chair, NDMRB.
E. The NDMRB shall not provide advice as a group, but rather, all advice is forwarded by individual members to the Chair, NDMRB.

2.17.2 Responsibilities.
  A. Chair.
    1) Receives general program policy guidance, excluding medical guidance, from the NDPM.
    2) Consults with medical experts on medical-related issues for consideration by the NDMRB when requested or deemed necessary.
    3) Summarizes all input from the NDMRB and reports findings and recommendations to the NDPM.
    4) Seeks consultation from an undersea or hyperbaric physician before a decision is rendered when circumstances or the situation does not allow for input from the membership of the NDMRB and the Chair is not a physician.
  B. NDMRB Members.
    1) Recommend medical policy and changes in medical operating procedures that will foster a safer and more efficient diving program.
    2) Review diver's medical qualifications forwarded by the NDP DMO to assess application of the NDP's medical evaluation criteria or other issues raised by the NDPM, NDCSB, or Chair, NDMRB.
    3) Review appeals from divers who are medically disqualified from diving and provide medical opinions and recommendations to the Chair.
    4) Provide medical reviews of diving incidents as requested by the Chair, NDMRB.

2.17.3 Qualifications.
  A. Chair.
    1) Federal employee or a member of a uniformed service.
    2) NOAA certified SCUBA diver.
    3) Complete a NOAA-approved DMO course.
    4) Must be a physician (MD/DO), NP, or PA.
  B. NDMRB members.
    1) Complete a NOAA-approved DMO course, and
    2) Be a physician with expertise in undersea or hyperbaric medicine.

2.18   NOAA Diving Technical Advisory Committee

2.18.1 General.
  A. The NOAA Diving Technical Advisory Committee is a standing committee of individuals outside of the agency with varying backgrounds and specialties in diving that advises the NDP on various operational and technical issues.
  B. Members of the committee are appointed by the NDCSB.
  C. The committee shall not provide advice as a group, but rather, all advice is forwarded by individual members to the Chair, NDCSB, through the NDPM.

2.18.2 Responsibilities.
  A. Review unique or specialized diving projects, equipment, and techniques; and provide comments on their safety and feasibility to the NDCSB.
  B. Provide comments to the NDCSB on proposed new diving equipment, regulations, policies, and procedures affecting the NDP.

2.18.3 Qualifications. Possess specialized knowledge or experience in diving.

SECTION 3: SCIENTIFIC DIVER CERTIFICATION AND TRAINING

3.1 Scientific Diver Certification Requirements

3.1.1 Prerequisites. Candidates for NOAA scientific diver certification must provide proof of the following:
   A. SCUBA diving certification, above the basic entry level, from a nationally, or internationally recognized, diver training agency;
   B. Rescue Diver certification, or equivalent as determined by the NDCSB, from a nationally or internationally recognized diver training agency;
   C. A minimum of 25 logged dives;
   D. Cardio-pulmonary resuscitation, including adult AED;
   E. First Aid (American Red Cross, American Heart Association or equivalent); and
   F. Oxygen administration (by a NOAA-approved agency).

3.1.2 Medical Clearance.
   A. All NOAA divers must successfully pass a NOAA diving physical examination and drug test prior to beginning the NOAA Scientific Diver certification process.
   B. Specific physical examination requirements are briefly described in Section 6 and covered in detail in the NOAA Diving Medical Standards and Procedures Manual which can be viewed and downloaded from the NDC website at www.ndc.noaa.gov.
   C. Physical exams must be completed by a credentialed provider (must be an MD, Doctor of Osteopathic Medicine (DO), NP, or PA), preferably with hyperbaric training.
   D. All physical exams shall be submitted directly to and approved by the NDP DMO.

3.1.3 Voluntary Drug Testing.
   A. The use of illegal drugs can dramatically affect the physical and mental condition of divers; which in turn can affect their abilities to make sound decisions underwater.
   B. As a condition for becoming a NOAA Diver, individuals not already in drug testing designated positions must:
      1) Submit to a voluntary drug test, and
      2) Volunteer for unannounced random testing in accordance with the Department of Commerce (DOC) Drug Free Workplace Plan and Guide.
   C. A verified positive drug test for any individual for which diving is included in their position descriptions may result in denial of initial employment, or if already employed, termination of employment.
   D. A verified positive drug test for any employees for which diving is not included in their position descriptions will result in denial of initial diving certification, or if already certified to dive, termination of NOAA diving privileges.
   E. Specific information on the drug testing program is outlined in the DOC Drug-Free Workplace Plan and the DOC Drug and Alcohol-Free Workplace Testing Guide; both of which can be downloaded at hr.commerce.gov.

3.1.4 Swim Test.
   A. General.
      1) All NOAA diver candidates must successfully pass the NOAA Swim Test prior to undergoing initial NOAA Scientific Diver certification.
      2) All swim test skills are to be completed in one (1) pool session and without the use of swimming aids (i.e., mask, fins, snorkel, or flotation devices).
      3) Completion of swim test shall be documented on the NOAA Scientific Diver Skill Checklist (Appendix 10), signed and dated by the NOAA Instructor.

B. NOAA Swim Test requirements include:
1) Swim 550 yards (500 meters) on the surface without stopping in under 15 minutes;
2) Swim 25 yards (22 meters) underwater without surfacing and without pushing off from the wall of the pool; and
3) Tread water for 30 minutes without any flotation aids.

3.1.5 Training.
A. General.
1) All scientific training dives conducted by employees and contract, reciprocity, and volunteer divers under the auspices of the NDP that are undertaken in furtherance of *scientific diving* may be conducted consistent with the standards outlined in this Manual provided the requirements for the scientific exemption outlined in 29 CFR § 1910.401(a)(2)(iv) are followed.
2) Scientific training dives are not required to comply with the commercial dive standards at 29 CFR § 1910 *et seq.* provided the dives are not combined with any element comprising a working or commercial dive.
3) NOAA UDSs are responsible for determining whether or not a dive can be performed under the OSHA Scientific Exemption (29 CFR § 1910.401(a)(2)(iv)) based on review of the dive plan and the credentials of the divers involved. Procedures associated with this responsibility are outlined in Section 1.1.4 of this Manual.
4) Documentation of completion.
   a) Successful completion of the academic and practical portions of the NOAA Scientific Diver Training Program shall be documented on the Student Evaluation Record by the NOAA Instructor and forwarded to the NDPM.
   b) The NDPM will review the form for compliance with NDP requirements and if complete, issue a NOAA Scientific Diver certification.
B. Academic Instruction.
1) Students must complete all material included in the NOAA Scientific Diver Student Study Guide.
2) Topics
   a) Physics laws and practice problems;
   b) Physiology;
   c) NOAA diving equipment;
   d) NOAA diving standards;
   e) NOAA diving skills and techniques;
   f) Dive planning;
   g) U.S. Navy Decompression Tables;
   h) Hazardous aquatic life;
   i) Emergency procedures;
   j) Dive preparation, pre-dive checks, and equipment set-up; and
   k) Post-dive information recording.
3) Students must pass all written examinations with a minimum score of 80 percent:
4) Candidates failing to obtain a passing mark on the exam should:
   a) Review the missed questions with the instructor; or
   b) Review or entirely repeat the appropriate sections in the student study guide
5) After appropriate remediation, as determined by the instructor, students can take a make-up exam for the topics they failed to pass.

6) Completion of academic instruction shall be documented on the NOAA Scientific Diver Training Course Student Evaluation Record (Appendix 11), signed and dated by the NOAA Instructor.

C. Practical Instruction.

1) Students must demonstrate successful completion of all skills, per performance criteria specified in the NOAA Scientific Diver Student Study Guide, in a pool and open-water environment.

2) In additional to basic scuba skills, students must also demonstrate proficiency in the following NOAA-specific skills and equipment:
   a) NOAA Reserve Air Supply System;
   b) Buddy breathing; and
   c) NOAA Standardized Equipment and configuration.

3) Completion of practical instruction shall be documented on the NOAA Scientific Diver Skill Checklist (Appendix 10), signed and dated by the NOAA Instructor.

4) Instructors may allow students who fail to complete a skill or exercise to repeat them until they demonstrate adequate performance.

3.2 Recognition of Non-NOAA Dive Certifications

3.2.1 General.

A. The NDCSB may accept non-NOAA dive certifications if it is determined that the certification is equivalent to, or greater than, NOAA certification.

B. The NDCSB will ultimately determine equivalency of non-NOAA dive certifications (e.g., commercial or military dive training and experience) towards meeting NOAA requirements.

3.2.2 Requirements. At a minimum, candidates for equivalency must:

A. Meet requirements outlined in Section 3.1;

B. Pass a written examination;

C. Complete NOAA-specific training as determined by the NDCSB; and complete skills check out (Open Water Evaluation) with the UDS, or designee.

3.3 Depth Limitations

3.3.1 Initial limitation. Although the nominal depth to which NOAA divers are certified is 130 fsw, all newly certified NOAA divers shall be limited to a maximum depth of 60 fsw until approved to dive deeper by the UDS.

3.3.2 Certification to Dive Deeper than 130 fsw.

A. A diver holding a 130 fsw certificate may be certified to a depth greater than 130 fsw after successfully completing a NDCSB-approved deep-diving training program.

B. Scientific dives requiring in-water decompression must be pre-approved by the NDCSB.

3.4   Maintaining Certification

3.4.1   General. In order to maintain active dive status, NOAA Scientific Divers must complete the requirements outlined below. Failure to do so may result in temporary suspension of diving privileges.

3.4.2   Dive Proficiency Requirements.
   A.   In order to maintain dive certification, NOAA divers must log a minimum of three (3) dives during each quarter of the calendar year.
   B.   Proficiency dives conducted by employees and contract, reciprocity, and volunteer divers undertaken in the furtherance of science may be conducted per standards outlined in this Manual.
   C.   Scientific proficiency dives are not required to comply with the commercial dive standards at 29 CFR § 1910 *et seq.* provided the dives are not combined with any element comprising a working or commercial dive.
   D.   NOAA UDSs or designees are responsible for determining whether a dive can be performed under the OSHA Scientific Exemption (29 CFR § 1910.401(a)(2)(iv)) based on review of the dive plan. Procedures associated with this responsibility are outlined in Section 1.1.4 of this Manual.

3.4.3   Medical Standards (See Section 6).

3.4.4   Emergency Care Training. NOAA divers and DPICs must remain current and provide proof of training to the UDS or designee in:
   A.   Adult CPR, including AED;
   B.   First Aid (American Red Cross, American Heart Association, or equivalent); and
   C.   Oxygen administration, which shall be completed annually and may be accomplished by completing the NOAA on-line refresher course followed by hands-on practice.

3.4.5   Annual Watermanship Assessment.
   A.   General.
      1) NOAA divers must pass the NOAA Diving Watermanship Assessment on an annual basis.
      2) Completion of this requirement is to be documented on the NDP Annual Watermanship Assessment form (Appendix15) by the UDS, or designee, and filed on site.
      3) Failure to meet the minimum watermanship assessment standards, or submit the form by the deadline, is cause for temporary suspension from diving.
   B.   The minimum requirements are:
      1) Swim 550 yards (500 meters) without stopping using mask, fins, and snorkel in less than 10 minutes.
      2) If using a wetsuit covering any part of the torso, the test must be completed in less than 12 minutes.
   C.   Responsibilities.
      1) Divers. All NOAA divers must pass the NOAA Diving Watermanship Assessment on an annual basis.
      2) Unit Diving Supervisors.
         a. Monitor administration of the NOAA Diving Watermanship Assessment on an annual basis.
         b. Suspend diving authorization of assigned divers not passing the NOAA Diving Watermanship Assessment.

       c. Advise the respective LODO/SODO of assigned divers who have not passed the NOAA Diving Watermanship Assessment.

       d. Delegate, as appropriate, administration of the NOAA Diving Watermanship Assessment to DMs or LDs.

    3) NOAA Line or Staff Office Diving Officers. Advise the NDPM of assigned divers who have not passed the NOAA Diving Watermanship Assessment.

    4) NOAA Diving Program Manager. Ensure NDC diver database reflects current diving status of all divers after notification by LODOs/SODO of assigned divers who have not passed the NOAA Diving Watermanship Assessment.

3.4.6 Physical Conditioning Training.

    A. Diving is physically demanding and it is imperative that both divers and managers recognize the need for a continual and aggressive exercise program that exceeds basic health maintenance standards.

    B. In order to help maintain appropriate fitness to dive, immediate supervisors may grant currently authorized NOAA divers up to 3 hours per week of official time to help maintain a conditioning level sufficient to pass the annual watermanship assessment.

    C. A variety of activities including, but not limited to, swimming, jogging, cross country skiing, cycling, walking, weight training, etc., are acceptable for maintaining sufficient condition for individuals required to dive.

3.4.7 Voluntary Drug Testing (Section 3.1.3).

3.4.8 Annual Training Requirement.

    A. General.

       1) All NOAA divers shall undergo annual refresher training consisting of in-water skills and academic instruction.

       2) Training shall be conducted over 2 separate days and documented in the Unit Training Log.

       3) Failure to comply with the Annual Training Requirements shall result in suspension of diving privileges.

    B. Requirements.

       1) In-water Training. The UDS or designee will conduct a checkout dive with each diver to assess in-water rescue and basic diving skills, including the retrieval of an unconscious diver from the surface of the water to a vessel or shore.

          a) Successful completion of skills is to be documented on the Rescue and Diving Skills Checkout Report (Appendix 6) by the UDS or designee.

          b) Copies of the most recent checkout reports must be kept by the UDS or designee for each diver and noted on the annual Diving Unit Assessment Checklist.

       2) Classroom Training. Complete academic instruction (self-study or instructor-lead) in the following topics:

          a) Oxygen administration;

          b) Recognition and treatment of diving accidents and injuries;

          c) 5-minute neurological examination;

          d) Rescue techniques;

          e) Diving accident management;

          f) NOAA Dive Tables for Multiple Air Dives; and

          g) NOAA Diving Standards, Policies, and Procedures.

3.5 Recertification

3.5.1 General. NOAA Scientific Divers whose dive certifications have lapsed due to lack of activity shall be temporarily suspended pending the completion of a recertification program.

3.5.2 Requirements.
A. 3-6 month lapse in conducting a dive:
1) If a diver does not complete a minimum of three (3) dives during a quarter, they must perform a training-only, basic checkout dive with the UDS or designee.
2) Based on the diver's performance during the checkout dive, the UDS may require additional academic or practical training in order to recertify.
3) Once the diver has met the recertification requirements prescribed by the UDS, the UDS will notify the NDC and the diver will be reauthorized to resume on-duty diving.
B. 6-12 month lapse in conducting a dive:
1) If a diver does not complete the required number of dives for a period of 6-12 months, the LODO/SODO is responsible for reauthorization.
2) Divers must complete a minimum of a training-only, basic checkout dive with the UDS or designee.
3) The NOAA Diving and Rescue Skills Checkout Report form (Appendix 6) must be completed.
4) The UDS will forward a copy of the Skills Checkout Form and a recommendation to the LODO/SODO for consideration.
5) The LODO/SODO will determine if the diver has met the recertification requirements and either authorize the diver to return to diving status or specify any additional requirements needed to reauthorize.
6) Once the diver is cleared to return to diving, the LODO/SODO will notify the NDC and the UDS that the diver may resume on-duty diving.
C. More than 12 month lapse. If a diver does not complete the required number of dives for a period of more than 12 months they must complete a refresher training program specified by the LODO/SODO.

3.6 Suspension and Revocation of Dive Certifications

3.6.1 General.
A. NOAA dive certifications may be temporarily suspended or permanently revoked for cause.
B. Temporary suspension of NOAA dive certification is typically issued for medical reasons or minor infractions of NOAA diving regulations, policies, or procedures.
C. Permanent revocation of dive certification is typically reserved for more serious conditions or violations of NOAA diving regulations, policies, or procedures.

3.6.2 Temporary Suspension.
A. Representative examples of situations and infractions leading to temporary suspension include, but are not limited to:
1) Failure of a diver to maintain minimum diving proficiency;
2) A lapse of CPR, including adult AED, first aid, and/or oxygen administration;
3) Failure to pass the Annual Watermanship Assessment;
4) The NDP DMO has concerns about findings on the Annual Medical Status Form;

5) Failure of a diver to pass a NOAA diving physical examination within the prescribed, age-based interval;
6) Failure of a diver to properly use or maintain NOAA-provided diving gear or support equipment;
7) Failure of a diver to comply with the policies and procedures of this Manual;
8) Reporting to the dive station mentally or physical impaired due to alcohol or other substance abuse;
9) An injury or condition that requires medical treatment beyond basic first aid; and
10) Surfacing from a dive with less than 500 pounds per square inch (psi).

B. Dive certifications can be temporarily suspended for cause by the NDPM, LODO/SODO, UDS, or on-site DM.

3.6.3 Permanent Revocation.
   A. Representative examples of situations and infractions leading to permanent revocation include, but are not limited to:
   1) Flagrant violation of NOAA standards, regulations, and policies; (e.g., diving solo without a tender, diving after notification of a lapsed physical exam without obtaining reauthorization),
   2) A not-fit-for-dive duty determination has been made by the Chair, NDMRB, following the conclusion of an Individualized Assessment (See NOAA Diving Medical Standards and Procedures Manual).
   B. Permanent revocation of dive certifications shall only be issued by the NDPM upon direction of the NDCSB.

3.6.4 Suspension or Revocation Appeal Process.
   A. Suspended divers may appeal the decision to the NDCSB within 30 days of receipt of notification.
   B. Terminated divers may appeal the decision to the OMAO Director within 30 days of receipt of notification.

SECTION 4: DIVING STANDARDS AND PROCEDURES

4.1 General

4.1.1 Qualification Requirements.
  A. For the purpose of performing operational scientific dives, or scientific training and proficiency dives consistent with this Manual, divers must meet the definition of a scientist listed in Section 1.1.2.
  B. Individuals not meeting the above requirement may participate in scientific dives as a "scientist-in-training" if the individual is appropriately briefed on the specific tasks to be performed during the dives by a scientist as defined in Section 1.1.2.

4.1.2 Diving experience or training.
  A. Each dive team member shall have the experience or training necessary to perform assigned tasks in a safe and healthful manner.
  B. Each dive-team member shall have experience or training in the following:
    1) The use of tools, equipment and systems relevant to assigned tasks;
    2) Techniques of the assigned diving mode; and
    3) Diving operations and emergency procedures.

4.1.3 Tasks Authorized.
  A. NOAA Scientific Divers can perform tasks commensurate with their certification level.
  B. Specialized training is required for tasks, equipment, techniques, and environments, including, but not limited to:
    1) Tasks involving the use of:
       a) Lift bags, and
       b) Towboard diving.
    2) Environments consisting of:
       a) Overhead obstructions;
       b) Blue-water;
       c) Restricted visibility;
       d) Currents greater than 1 kt; and
       e) Water temperatures below 50 degrees (F).
    3) Equipment:
       a) Drysuits;
       b) Full-face masks;
       c) Tethered SCUBA; and
       d) Surface-supplied.

4.1.4 Restrictions.
  A. Dive team members:
    1) Shall not engage in scientific diving operations under the auspices of the NDP unless they hold a current certification or specialized task endorsement for the type of tasks to be performed;
    2) Shall not be assigned tasks inconsistent with the individual's verifiable experience or training, except that limited additional tasks may be assigned to an individual undergoing training provided that these tasks are performed under the direct supervision of an experienced dive team member;
    3) Shall not perform advanced scientific-related skills in deep water until they have demonstrated these skills in shallow water (<60 fsw) to the satisfaction of the UDS or designee;

    4) Shall not be permitted to dive or be exposed to hyperbaric conditions for the duration of any temporary physical impairment or condition that is known to NOAA and is likely to adversely affect the safety or health of a dive team member;

    5) Shall not be permitted to dive for the duration of any known medical condition, which is likely to adversely affect the safety and health of the diver or other dive team members.

    6) Shall not be exposed to hyperbaric conditions against their will, except when necessary to complete decompression or treatment procedures; and

    7) Who are exposed to or control the exposure of others to hyperbaric conditions shall be trained in diving-related physics and physiology.

B. Hours of Operation.

    1) The normal work schedule for personnel engaged in diving activities should not exceed 12 hours during any 24 hour period.

    2) A minimum rest period of 8 continuous hours is required for all divers during each 24 hour period.

    3) This standard is waived for watchstanders on vessels with schedules of 6 hours on-duty and 6 hours off-duty; however, they shall have a minimum rest period of 8 hours during each 24 hour period.

C. Consecutive Days of Diving.

    1) The DM, or LD, in charge of the dive operations has full authority to institute a mandatory day of rest (i.e., 24-hours without diving or strenuous activity) for individual divers, or the entire dive team, if in his/her opinion, continued diving would compromise the safety of the divers.

    2) Unless approved by the DM, or LD, a mandatory day of rest will be instituted after 10 consecutive days of diving.

4.1.5 Participation in Non-NOAA Scientific Diving Operations.

A. NOAA divers may participate in an official capacity in non-NOAA scientific diving operations with agencies with which NOAA has established diving reciprocity agreements pending approval from their UDS, receipt of a letter of reciprocity from the NDC, and LO program authorization.

B. NOAA divers may also participate in an official capacity in non-NOAA scientific diving operations with agencies without established diving reciprocity agreements with NOAA provided the divers comply with the NOAA diving regulations, policies, and procedures specified in this Manual, the operation is approved by the NDCSB and a Memorandum of Understanding has been established with the receiving organization by the NDPM.

4.1.6 Diver Responsibility.

A. It is the responsibility of the diver to terminate the dive, without fear of penalty, whenever they feel it is unsafe to continue the dive, unless to do so compromises the safety of another diver already in the water.

B While the employer has ultimate responsibility for safety in the workplace, divers are responsible for their own safety and share responsibility for the safety of their buddy. Part of this responsibility is the requirement to refuse to dive if in the diver's judgment:

    1) Conditions are unsafe or unfavorable;

    2) They are not in good physical or mental condition for diving; or

    3) They would violate the dictates of their training or the NDP regulations, policies or procedures.

B. Divers are also responsible for:
1) Reporting any signs or symptoms of diving maladies to the DPIC, DM, or LD;
2) Reporting any unsafe acts that could jeopardize their or their fellow divers' health and safety; and
3) Using and maintaining their NOAA-issued diving equipment properly.

4.1.7 Unit Inspections.
A. All NOAA diving units will conduct an annual self-inspection using the NDP Unit Diving Assessment Checklist which can be found at www.ndc.noaa.gov.
B. Periodically (frequency to be determined), NOAA diving units will also be inspected by the NOAA Diving Safety Officer, or his designee, as part of the Diving Unit Safety Assessment (DUSA) program.
C. It is anticipated that a DUSA inspection will include all unit specific applicable items listed in the NDP Unit Diving Assessment Checklist.
D. Units found to be deficient may be suspended from diving by the NDSO, NDPM, or LODO/SODO until discrepancies are corrected.

4.1.8 Pay for Performing Dive Duties.
A. NAO 202-532A, Pay for Performing Dive Duties, establishes guidance for paying NOAA employees additional compensation for performing dive duties.
B. NOAA employees are entitled to receive dive pay for official dives performed.

4.2 Pre-Dive Procedures

4.2.1 General. The requirements outlined in this section shall be completed prior to each diving operation, unless otherwise specified.

4.2.2 Dive Planning and Approval.
A. A formal written dive plan shall be completed and submitted to the appropriate UDS, or designee, for approval and signature prior to each separate dive operation.
B. All dive planning shall be conducted in accordance with the NOAA Dive Operation Plan (Appendix 3), which can be downloaded from the NDC website at www.ndc.noaa.gov.
C. If a dive operation is deemed "intensive," as outlined in the NDP Dive Plan Review Policy Algorithm (see Appendix 8), then the UDS shall submit a copy of the dive plan to the LODO/SODO to determine the need for an on-site chamber.
D. The plan should be based on the skill level of the least experienced member of the dive team.
E. The UDS shall keep a copy of the dive plan on file for 24 hours after conclusion of the dive operation, and shall provide a copy of the approved dive plan to the DM or LD responsible for overseeing the dive.
F. All dives conducted during duty hours, must comply with the dive plan requirements.
G. Dive plans are required for each unique diving operation.
H. Multi-day operations with similar objectives, tasks and locations may be combined on one (1) dive plan.
I. Minor changes in dive plans may be made on-site by the DM or LD; however, any significant changes must be re-approved by the UDS or designee.
J. Once a dive plan is approved by the UDS, or designee, it is to be submitted electronically to the following address: ndp.diveplans@noaa.gov.

K. Dive plans involving diving equipment other than open circuit SCUBA, breathing mixtures other than air or Nitrox, or decompression dive profiles must be pre-approved by the NDCSB and shall include, but are not limited to, the following elements:
1) Overview of the operations;
2) Goals, objectives, and tasks to be accomplished;
3) Nature of tasks (i.e., scientific versus working);
4) Description and location of dive site;
5) Names, affiliations, roles/responsibilities, and qualifications of all participants;
6) Schedule of operations;
7) Description of equipment and facilities;
8) Logistical arrangements and considerations;
9) Normal and emergency diving procedures;
10) Diving Emergency Assistance Plan (DEAP); and
11) Supporting documents, permits, and required forms.

4.2.3 Diving Emergency Assistance Plan (DEAP).
A. A DEAP must be submitted to the appropriate UDS or designee, for review and approval on an annual basis or when the information on the DEAP might change (i.e., geographically or seasonally).
B. A DEAP is filed with a dive plan at ndp.diveplans@noaa.gov in accordance with the above.
C. All dive accident plans shall be prepared in accordance with the NOAA Diving Emergency Assistance Plan Template (Appendix 4) which can be downloaded from the NDC website at www.ndc.noaa.gov
D. Once approved, the plan shall be available to all divers and support personnel at the site of the diving operation.
E. The UDS shall keep the DEAP on file for the duration of the dive operation.
F. DEAPs can be for specific time frames or entire regions if there are no changes in chamber locations or means of evacuation.
G. A list shall be kept at the dive location of the telephone or call numbers of the following:
1) Closest primary and secondary operational hyperbaric chamber and the attending physician (if not at the dive location);
2) Accessible hospitals;
3) NOAA-approved Diving Medical Officers;
4) Available means of transportation;
5) Divers Alert Network (DAN); and
6) The nearest U.S. Coast Guard facility.

4.2.4 Pre-Dive Safety Briefings.
A. Prior to any dive, a dive safety briefing shall be conducted by the DM or LD.
B. At a minimum the briefing shall include:
1) The tasks to be undertaken;
2) Safety procedures for the diving mode;
3) Any unusual hazards or environmental conditions likely to affect the safety of the diving operation;
4) Any modifications to operating procedures necessitated by the specific diving operation;
5) General goals and objectives;

6) Dive plan (maximum depth, maximum bottom time, and 500 psi ending cylinder pressure;

7) Entry and exit location and procedures;

8) Descent, on-bottom, and ascent procedures; and

9) Emergency and accident management procedures.

4.2.5 Pre-Dive Checklist.

A. A formal written pre- and post-dive checklist must be completed by the on-site DM or LD for each diving day.

B. Use the NOAA Pre and Post Dive Checklist (Appendix 5), which can be downloaded from the NDC website at www.ndc.noaa.gov.

1) The checklist includes a signature and date block that is to be completed by the individual completing the checklist.

2) The checklist will be kept at the dive site or unit level for 24 hours following the dive, unless an incident has occurred in which case it will be kept indefinitely.

4.2.6 Fitness to Dive.

A. Prior to commencement of dive operation the DM or LD shall:

1) Assess each dive team member's current state of physical and mental readiness to dive and deny diving privileges to anyone deemed unfit to dive; and

2) Inform the dive team members that physical problems or adverse physiological effects should be verbally reported to the DM or LD.

B. Divers should refrain from alcohol consumption for a minimum of 12 hours prior to diving and 4 hours after diving.

C. Divers exhibiting any effects of alcohol or substance abuse shall not be permitted to dive and will have their diving certification temporarily suspended or permanently revoked from diving pending review by the NDCSB.

4.2.7 Emergency Equipment and Supplies.

A. First aid kit. The following items shall be available at the dive location:

1) A physician approved first aid kit, appropriate for the diving or chamber operation, and with current medications (Appendix 9); and

2) A first aid handbook from the American Red Cross, American Heart Association or equivalent.

B. Oxygen resuscitator.

1) Positive pressure ventilator or a bag-type manual resuscitator with transparent mask capable of ventilating an unconscious victim.

2) Sufficient quantity of oxygen to supply a diver for:

a) The time required to transport them to a higher-level medical care facility; or

b) 12 hours, whichever occurs first.

Oxygen cylinders shall be maintained within current hydrostatic test date.

Oxygen kits shall be stowed in a clean, protected and clearly labeled space.

C. Automated External Defibrillator (AED). An AED shall be available at the dive site, when practical, and only operated by trained personnel.

D. Backboard. A backboard, in good working condition, shall be available at the dive site when practical.

4.2.8 Equipment Inspection.

A. All diver-worn and related support equipment and systems shall be inspected and tested prior to each dive by the dive team members.

B. Each diver shall conduct a functional check of their diving equipment in the presence of their dive buddy or tender.

C. The DM or LD shall conduct a final safety check of each diver's gear before allowing divers to enter the water.

D. Any equipment in questionable condition shall be removed from service immediately and clearly labeled in order to preclude its use.

E. Unless approved by the LODO/SODO, all dive equipment shall be worn in the configuration depicted in Appendix 7.

F. Any LODO/SODO-approved deviation from the standard SEP gear or configuration shall be in written form and kept at the unit level by the UDS.

G. Non-SEP dive equipment shall be inspected by the UDS, or designee.

H. Maintenance records on non-SEP dive equipment shall be kept at the unit level by the UDS.

I. An annual SEP equipment inventory shall be conducted by each diver.

4.2.9 Warning Signals.

A. When diving in areas capable of supporting marine traffic, a red and white "diver down" sport diving flag, appropriately sized for the vessel used, shall be displayed at the dive location in a manner which allows all-round visibility, and shall be illuminated during night diving operations.

B. Depending on the situation, the DM or LD may choose to also display the code flag "A" at the dive location.

4.2.10 Hyperbaric Chamber Requirement.

A. NOAA hyperbaric chambers shall be equipped and operated in accordance with Sections 6.11 and 7.26 NWDSSM.

B. No-Decompression Dives.

1) Dive operations conducted within the U.S. Navy (USN) no-decompression limits may require access to a hyperbaric chamber within 6 hours of the dive location if deemed "intensive" in nature.

2) If a dive operation is deemed "intensive," as outlined in the NDP Dive Plan Review Policy Algorithm (see Appendix 8), then the UDS shall submit a copy of the dive plan to the LODO/SODO to determine the need for an on-site chamber.

C. Decompression dives must be pre-approved by the NDCSB and conducted per Section 8 of this Manual.

4.2.11 Diver Recall Capability. Topside personnel must be capable of recalling divers during all diving operations.

4.3 Diving Procedures and Requirements

4.3.1 Water Entry and Exit.

A. A means shall be provided to assist all divers entering and exiting the water.

B. The means provided for exiting the water shall extend below the water surface.

C. A means shall be provided to extract an unconscious diver from the water.

D. A small boat and qualified operator shall be used to deploy or retrieve divers when dives are conducted beyond a comfortable swimming distance from shore, in areas of strong current, and/or arduous egress.

E. The propulsion system (e.g., propeller, jet drive) of the vessel shall be disengaged before divers enter or exit the water.

4.3.2   Communications.
   A. An operational, two-way surface communication system (e.g., VHF radio, cell phone) shall be available at the dive location to obtain emergency assistance.
   B. An operational two-way voice communication (wireless or hard-wire) system shall be used when:
      1) Diving in surface-supplied mode, between each surface-supplied diver and a dive team member at the dive location, and
      2) Diving in tethered SCUBA mode, between solo tethered diver and a topside tender.
   C. Diving operations shall be coordinated with other activities in the vicinity which are likely to interfere with the diving operation.

4.3.3   Supervisor Dive Log. A dive log will be kept at the dive location in accordance with Section 12.1.5.

4.3.4   Decompression Tables and Procedures. A set of NOAA-approved decompression tables (as appropriate for the breathing gases used) shall be at the dive location.

4.3.5   Buddy System for SCUBA Diving.
   A. All diving activities shall assure adherence to accepted standards of the buddy system for SCUBA diving.
   B. Except under emergency conditions, or when tethered or line-tended as a standby diver, the buddy system, consisting of a minimum of two (2) comparably equipped divers in constant visual or physical communication with one another, is required.
   C. The buddy system is based upon mutual assistance, especially in the case of an emergency; therefore, SCUBA divers shall remain close enough to each other during dives to render immediate assistance in an emergency.
   D. When conditions are such that the probability of separation of divers is high, such as low visibility, some form of direct physical contact between divers should be maintained (Section 4.9).
   E. If separated during a dive, divers shall try to re-establish contact for no more than 1 minute and if unsuccessful, immediately begin a controlled ascent to the surface.

4.3.6   Safety Stops.
   A. For all no-decompression dives conducted deeper than 60 fsw a precautionary safety stop should be performed at a depth between 15 feet and 20 feet for 3-5 minutes.
   B. The time spent at a safety stop need not be added to the diver's total bottom time.
   C. If sea conditions or breathing gas supply are such that safety stops cannot be performed safely, they may be omitted.

4.3.7   Reserve Air Supply System Requirement.
   A. A diver-carried reserve breathing gas supply consisting of an independent reserve cylinder with a separate regulator shall be worn by each diver for all scientific dives conducted:
      1) Outside the no-decompression limits;
      2) In overhead environments where direct ascent to the surface is prevented by a natural or man-made obstruction;
      3) In conditions of low visibility where the diver cannot read his cylinder pressure gauge;
      4) In enclosed or physically confined spaces;

5) Deeper than 100 feet;

7) By solo divers being line-tended; and

8) When deemed appropriate by the DM or LD.

B. The reserve supply shall be of sufficient quantity to allow the diver to reach the surface and kept in the closed position prior to the dive.

C. Systems that may be used to meet the above requirement include:

1) NOAA Reserve Air Supply System (RASS) for depths to 130 fsw,

2) SpareAir® (3 Ft^3 minimum) for depths ≤ 30 feet.

D. The NOAA RASS shall be mounted and configured per diagram in Appendix 7. Deviations from the mounting and configuration diagram must be approved by the diver's LODO/SODO and must comply with the following minimum standards:

1) The tank valve must be easily accessible and not be blocked by any other diver-worn equipment.

2) The high-pressure hose must be of sufficient length to allow the diver to easily read the HP gauge.

3) The second-stage hose must be of sufficient length to easily reach the mouth and to allow for head movement (rotation) from shoulder to shoulder.

4) If a longer hose is used for the second stage, it must be either a) stored where it can be accessed easily, b) worn on a necklace (Tech style) or c) the second stage must be fastened with a proven quick release mechanism (octo-holder etc.) to the Buoyancy Compensator Device (BCD).

5) The RASS cylinder must be securely mounted in a manner that allows for easy removal underwater.

6) The RASS cylinder must remain in the 'off' position during the dive, unless the second-stage regulator hose is equipped with an in-line shutoff valve and in-line relief valve.

7) If Buoyancy Compensator Devices (BCD) cam-bands are used for securing RASS cylinder bracket assemblies, the mounting must not interfere with the intended purpose of the cam-bands.

8) The RASS cylinder on/off valve must be uniquely identified/configured so that it is easily distinguished, visually or tactually, from the cylinder yoke screw.

9) Unless authorized by the LODO, RASS cylinders shall be mounted either on the diver's right side (e.g., BCD or cylinder) or in front at belt level.

E. Distribution

1) The NDC will not issue RASS to NOAA Science Divers as a standard piece of dive equipment under the Standardized Equipment Program.

2) Each UDS shall determine the minimum number of RASS required for their unit.

3) RASS shall be available for divers to "checkout" during scientific, working, training, or proficiency dives, or as needed.

4) Excess RASS shall be returned to the NDC to eliminate the need for yearly servicing of unused equipment and avoid being assessed additional SEP fees.

4.3.8 Minimum Cylinder Pressure Requirement.

A. All divers shall frequently check the pressure remaining in their SCUBA cylinders during dives and periodically compare the amounts with those of their dive buddies.

B. All pre- and post-dive SCUBA cylinder pressures will be logged.

C. Any recorded pressure of less than 500 psi will result in temporary suspension of dive privileges for that individual diver until the on-site DM or LD investigates the matter.

D. If it is determined that the infraction is an unjustified violation of the 500 psi rule, the individual will not be permitted to resume diving until cleared by the diver's UDS.

    E. If it is determined that the cause of the infraction is justified (e.g., to render emergency assistance to a dive buddy), then the DM or LD may lift the suspension and allow the individual to resume diving.

    F. Repeated violation of the minimum pressure rule, even if justified, may result in temporary suspension pending review by the UDS.

    G. The UDS will report all violations of the 500 psi minimum policy to the LODO/SODO.

4.3.9 Topside Support.

    A. Unless specifically authorized by the UDS, a topside support person must be available at the dive site and ready, willing and able to render assistance in an emergency. This person must be familiar with the dive activities being conducted and physically able to assist in the recovery of an injured diver.

    B. For all dives conducted beyond a comfortable swimming distance from shore, in areas of strong current, arduous egress or outside the no-decompression limits, a support boat and qualified operator is required to be in the water and ready to render assistance as needed.

    C. The small boat operator can serve as topside support.

    D. The DM/LD may require additional topside support personnel based on the conditions anticipated.

4.3.10 Standby Diver(s).

    A. Standby diver(s) shall be configured per Appendix 7 and ready to enter the water within 1 minute of notification for dives:

        1) Conducted deeper than 100 feet or outside the no-decompression limits; or

        2) Conducted in overhead environments where direct ascent to the surface is limited (e.g., hulls of ships, wreck penetrations, ice); or

        3) Involving tethered/line-tended SCUBA diving by a solo diver; or

        4) Deemed appropriate by the DM or LD of the dive operation.

    B. Depending on the situation, options for standby divers include:

        1) A buddy team of SCUBA divers;

        2) A solo line-tended SCUBA diver; or

        3) A solo tethered SCUBA diver with voice communications.

    C. Unless called to action, the standby diver must remain on the surface during dives.

    D. DMs may serve as standby divers, but if they are deployed, another topside support person must take their place.

    E. All efforts should be taken to minimize physical and environmental stressors on the standby diver(s) as they perform their duties.

4.3.11 Termination of Dive.

    A. Diver Responsibility. It is the responsibility of the diver to terminate the dive, without fear of penalty, whenever he/she feels it is unsafe to continue the dive, unless to do so compromises the safety of another diver already in the water.

    B. Minimum Cylinder Surface Pressure. The dive shall be terminated while there is still sufficient SCUBA cylinder pressure to permit the diver and their buddy to safely reach the surface with at least 500 psi in their cylinder(s), including decompression time, or to safely reach an additional air source at the decompression station with at least 500 psi in their cylinder(s).

    C. A dive shall be terminated when:

        1) A diver, DM, LD, or vessel captain requests termination;

        2) A diver fails to respond correctly to communications or signals from a dive team member;

    3) A diver loses visual or physical contact with his dive buddy for more than 1 minute;

    4) A diver begins to use a reserve breathing gas supply, other than during a drill;

    5) A diver is forced to use an alternate air source, other than during a drill;

    6) A diver uses buddy breathing, other than during a drill;

    7) An emergency recall is activated from the surface;

    8) There is an equipment failure that may compromise the safety of the diving operation;

    9) Conditions become unsafe for divers or support personnel; or

    10) The standby diver(s) has been deployed to assist any diver.

4.3.12 Performance of Working Tasks.

    A. NOAA Scientific Divers may perform working dives utilizing dive equipment and work techniques listed in this Manual (e.g., small lift-bags, light hand tools, photography), as long as they have received proper instruction in the equipment to be used and work to be performed.

    B. Such dives are not scientific in nature and therefore, must comply with the NOAA Working Diving Standards and Safety Manual.

    C. NOAA Scientific Divers are prohibited from performing dives requiring equipment and/or work techniques not identified in this Manual.

    D. Unit Diving Supervisors are responsible for determining whether or not a dive can be performed under the OSHA Scientific Exemption (29 CFR § 1910.401(a)(2)(iv)) based on review of the dive plan and the credentials of the divers involved.

4.4 Post-Dive Procedures

4.4.1 Precautions.

    A. After the completion of any dive, the DM or LD shall:

      1) Check the physical condition of each diver;

      2) Instruct the divers to report any physical problems or adverse physiological effects including symptoms of decompression sickness along with any equipment malfunctions; and

      3) Remind divers to remain together for 30 minutes and monitor their dive buddies.

    B. For any dive outside the no-decompression limits, DMs or LDs shall instruct the divers to remain awake and in the vicinity of the hyperbaric chamber which is at the dive location for at least 1 hour after the dive (including decompression or treatment as appropriate).

4.4.2 Post-Dive Debriefing and Checklist.

    A. Following each dive a debriefing shall be conducted including at a minimum, but not limited to:

      1) Dive profile information (maximum depth, maximum bottom time and ending cylinder pressure);

      2) Completion of goals and objectives;

      3) Suggestions for next team of divers;

      4) Location and contact information of a hyperbaric chamber which is ready for use; and

      5) Potential hazards regarding flying or ascending to altitudes in excess of 1000 feet within 24 hours after completion of a dive.

B. Post Dive Checklist. Complete the Post Dive section of the NOAA Pre and Post Dive Checklist and file for 24 hours following the completion of dive operations, unless there is an incident in which case it shall be kept indefinitely.

4.4.3　Dive Incident Reporting and Investigation.
　　　A. Dive-related injuries requiring medical treatment beyond basic first aid shall be reported, investigated and documented as prescribed in Section 12 of this Manual.
　　　B. All 'near-miss' or "close call" incidents that could have resulted in a fatality or serious injury to a dive team member shall be reported and documented in accordance with the policies and procedures outlined in Section 12 of this Manual.

4.4.4　Post-Dive Health Considerations.
　　　A. Divers shall limit pre- and post-dive exertion due to the potential of bubble formation that could lead to decompression sickness, and
　　　B. Report all injuries, and signs or symptoms of hyperbaric maladies to the DM or LD as soon as they are experienced.

4.5　SCUBA Diving Mode

4.5.1　General.
　　　A. SCUBA diving mode, as distinct from surface-supplied mode, consists of two methods: free-swimming and tethered.
　　　B. All SCUBA operations conducted using tethered or line-tended divers (including standby divers) shall be conducted from a moored or fixed platform (i.e., no live boating).
　　　C. A team of divers or a tended diver shall be stationed at the underwater point of entry when diving is conducted in enclosed or physically confining spaces.
　　　D. Divers trained in specialized diving techniques and equipment (e.g., line and tethered SCUBA diving, drysuits) must maintain annual proficiency in the types of equipment and procedures for which they are authorized. Failure to maintain proficiency may result in loss of authority to perform such dives.

4.5.2　Manning Requirements. The minimum personnel required to conduct a SCUBA dive:
　　　A. Non-tethered, free swimming (minimum 4).

Divers	2
Topside Support[1]	1
Standby Diver[1,2]	1
Total	4

Divers	2
Topside Support[1]	1
Standby Diver[1,3]	2
Total	5

　　　B. Tethered (minimum of 3).

Divers	1
Topside Support[1]	1
Standby Diver[1,2]	1
Total	3

Divers	1
Topside Support[1]	1
Standby Diver[1,3]	2
Total	4

Notes:
[1] Topside Support and Standby Divers are only required in certain situations. Refer to Section 4.3.10 for Topside Support and Section 4.3.10 for Standby Divers.
[2] The standby diver must be a trained, line-tended individual.
[3] Line-tending not required if two standby buddy divers are used.

4.5.3 Limits. SCUBA diving shall not be conducted:
A. At depths deeper than 130 fsw or outside the no-decompression limits unless a hyperbaric chamber is accessible within 2 hours of the dive site and with pre-approval of the NDCSB.
B. Against currents exceeding 1 knot unless line-tended.
C. From an un-moored vessel when sea conditions prevent safe deployment, retrieval or tracking of divers.

4.5.4 Breathing Gas Supplies.
A. Diver-carried breathing gas supplies shall only be used for:
   1) Breathing purposes;
   2) Inflating BCDs and variable-volume drysuits; and
   3) Lift bags or surface marker buoys of less than 25 lbs positive buoyancy.
B. Lift-bags of more than 25 lbs positive buoyancy may only be inflated from a separate diver carried or surface supplied gas source, other than that used for life support.
C. A diver-carried reserve air supply system of sufficient quantity to allow the diver to reach the surface or another appropriate gas supply shall be worn as specified in Section 4.3.8.

4.5.5 Use of Dive Computers.
A. Any commercially available dive computer may be used for no-decompression diving by completing a Dive Computer User Agreement, available from the NDC website.
B. Dive computers for decompression dives must be approved by the NDCSB.

4.6 Drysuit Diving

4.6.1 General.
A. NOAA divers wanting to use drysuits must complete formal training in the equipment and be certified by the NDPM.
B. Such training may be obtained from a number of sources including, but not limited to: NOAA, US military, academic institutions, and recreational agencies.
C. Experience may be substituted for formal training as determined by the NDPM.

4.6.2 Training. At a minimum, formal drysuit training shall include:
A. Academic instruction:
   1) Drysuit components;
   2) Equipment preparation and maintenance;
   3) Donning and doffing procedures;
   4) Weighting systems and usage; and
   5) Emergency procedures.
B. Practical instruction:
   1) Pool:
      a) Equipment preparation;
      b) Donning and doffing procedures;
      c) Disconnecting and reconnecting drysuit inflator hose;
      d) Buoyancy control; and
      e) Emergency procedures.
   2) Confined or open-water dives with an instructor:
      a) Emergency management for excess positive buoyancy;
      b) Ditching of weights; and

      c) Disconnecting and reconnecting drysuit inflator hose.

   3) Drysuit certification requires a minimum of five (5) open-water dives wearing a drysuit for a cumulative bottom time of at least 120 minutes.

4.6.3   Equipment.
   A. In addition to the standard SCUBA diving configuration listed in Section 5.3.1, NOAA drysuit divers shall also wear a weight-harness system with a quick-release mechanism requiring the use of only one hand.
   B. Ankle weights are optional except during initial drysuit training.
   C. A drysuit diver's buoyancy should be controlled by the suit itself while underwater; whereas, the BCD should only be used for surface flotation.
   D. The use of non-SEP-issued drysuits must be pre-approved by the UDS or designee based on inspection of the suit for condition and functionality.

4.6.4   Emergency Procedures.
   A. Loss of positive buoyancy:
     1) The diver should ditch one or both sides of his harness weights, terminate dive, and swim to the surface, and
     2) Once at surface, inflate the BCD.
   B. Excess positive buoyancy. The diver should, in order of preference:
     1) Swim down to compress air in suit to help reduce excess buoyancy;
     2) Roll to head-up position;
     3) Dump air from suit using exhaust valve;
     4) Dump air from suit at wrist or neck seals; or
     5) Flare-out to increase surface area to help slow ascent and exhale.
   C. Free-flowing suit inlet valve:
     1) Manually disconnect the inflator hose from suit.
     2) If ascending too quickly, follow instructions for excess positive buoyancy above.

4.7   Line-Tended SCUBA Diving

4.7.1   General.
   A. Line-tended SCUBA diving is a specialized diving technique whereby divers are connected to the surface via a strength member (line) managed by a trained individual topside.
   B. As defined by NOAA, line-tended diving does not utilize voice communications and, therefore, can only be used by standby divers.
   C. Each line-tended SCUBA diver must be tended by a separate tender.

4.7.2   Manning Requirements (Section 4.5.2).

4.7.3   Limits. Line-tended SCUBA diving is restricted to the same limits as non-tethered, free-swimming SCUBA mode (Section 4.5.3).

4.7.4   Equipment Requirements. In addition to standard SCUBA diving equipment, divers shall be tended with a strength member (line) capable of lifting the diver from the water.

4.7.5   Training Requirements.
   A. Academic instruction shall include, but not be limited to:
     1) Specialized equipment;

     2) Tending procedures;

     3) Communication procedures;

     4) Diving procedures; and

     5) Emergency procedures.

B. Practical instruction shall include, but not be limited to:

     1) Dressing procedures;

     2) Tending procedures; and

     3) Emergency procedures.

C. Non-divers may be trained as tenders and shall participate in the entire training session, minus the actual diving portion, outlined in this section. Academic instruction for line-tended training can be found at www.ndc.noaa.gov.

4.7.6 Tender Responsibilities.

A. Tenders shall ensure the diver receives proper care while topside.

B. While the diver is submerged, the tender handles the tending line and communicates with the diver via line-pull signals.

C. Line-tended divers and tenders may develop additional line pull signals, but all divers and tenders must know standard line signals adapted from the USN.

4.8 Tethered SCUBA with Voice Communications

4.8.1 General.

A. When conducting tethered SCUBA diving operations the diver shall be equipped with a life-line and two-way voice communications.

B. Standby divers may also be outfitted with two-way communication, but it is not mandatory.

4.8.2 Manning Requirements. (Section 4.5.2)

4.8.3 Limits. Tethered SCUBA diving is restricted to the same limits as non-tethered, free-swimming SCUBA mode. (Section 4.5.3)

4.8.4 Equipment Requirements.

A. In addition to standard SCUBA diving equipment, the following minimum items shall be included in a tethered SCUBA diving assembly:

     1) Demand breathing lightweight full-face mask with communications;

     2) Strength member tether with quick release snap shackle;

     3) Hardwired or wireless voice communications;

     4) Surface communications unit; and

     5) Man-rated safety harness for lifting the diver from the water.

B. Any deviation from the above requirements must be approved by the LODO/SODO.

4.8.5 Training.

A. Academic instruction shall include, but not be limited to:

     1) Tether equipment;

     2) Tending procedures;

     3) Communication procedures;

     4) Diving procedures; and

     5) Emergency procedures.

B. Practical instruction shall include, but not be limited to:

1) Pool or confined-water conditions:
   a) Dressing procedures;
   b) Diving procedures;
   c) Tending procedures; and
   d) Emergency procedures.
2) Open-water instruction shall include, but not be limited to a minimum of five (5) dives with a minimum cumulative bottom time of 150 minutes for certification.

C. Non-divers may be trained as surface tenders and shall participate in the entire training session, minus the actual diving portion, outlined in this section. Academic instruction for line-tended training can be found at www.ndc.noaa.gov.

4.8.6   Tender Responsibilities.
A. It is the tender's responsibility to ensure the diver receives proper care while topside.
B. While the diver is submerged, the tender handles the tether, maintains communications, and monitors diver's air usage by periodically requesting pressure readings from the diver.
C. The usual means of communications between diver and tender is by voice intercom. However, it is important that basic line signals be memorized and practiced so they will be recognized instantly in the event of intercom failure.
D. Dive teams may develop additional line pull signals, but all divers and tenders will know standard line signals adapted from the USN.

4.8.7   Emergency Procedures.
A. Loss of primary gas supply. The diver will switch to the reserve breathing supply, notify topside personnel, terminate the dive and follow their tether back to the surface.
B. Loss of voice communication. The diver will stop all activity, signal topside personnel via line-pull signals and begin ascent to the surface.
C. Entanglement.
   1) The diver will notify topside personnel via voice communications or line-pull signals and wait for assistance from the standby diver.
   2) If the standby is delayed or the diver is in jeopardy of running out of air, the diver can disconnect themselves from the tether and swim to the surface.
D. Flooded mask. If the diver is unable to purge a flooded mask, they will switch to the reserve breathing supply, notify topside personnel via line-pulls, terminate the dive and ascend to the surface.

4.8.8   Proficiency Requirements. In order to maintain tethered SCUBA diving certification, all trained divers and tenders must perform/tend at least one (1) tethered SCUBA dive every 12 months. Dives will be documented using the standard on-line dive log.

4.9   Diving in Low Visibility

4.9.1   General.
A. NOAA diving operations conducted in low visibility, as defined in Appendix 2 of this Manual, shall comply with the standards outlined below.
B. Where conditions are such that visual contact cannot be maintained, physical contact, either directly (holding hands) or indirectly (buddy line with quick-release), may be used to maintain buddy contact.

4.9.2 Requirements.
  A. All NOAA scuba divers shall be line-tended/tethered from the surface, or accompanied by another diver in the water in continuous visual or physical contact during the diving operations.
  B. Physical contact may include either direct physical touching or the use of a short buddy-line with quick-releases on both ends.
  C. NOAA divers shall be trained in both methods of maintaining contact.

4.9.3 Equipment.
  A. Equipment used for line-tending diver(s) in zero visibility shall comply with standards described in the <u>Procedures for Tending Standby Scuba Divers</u> presentation available for viewing at: www.ndc.noaa.gov/training/dive_tending_procedures/launcher.html.
  B. Buddy lines used to maintain tactile contact between two divers shall be limited to a maximum length of 6 feet and be secured to each diver in a manner that can be quickly released if required.

4.9.4 Responsibilities.
  A. NOAA DM.
    1) Determines when procedures for diving in low visibility must be initiated.
    2) Ensures all dive team members have completed line-tending training and the minimum required equipment to perform low-visibility diving is available.
    3) Determines which deployment protocol (Section 4.9.2A) to use to conduct the low-visibility dives.
  B. NOAA Unit Diving Supervisor. Appoints DMs to oversee and direct diving operations.

4.10   Blue-Water Diving

4.10.1 General.
  A. Blue-water diving is defined as diving conducted in any body of water in which there is no physical bottom within diving depth ranges, depth is deeper than diver certification, and/or depth is greater than breathing gas Maximum Operating Depth (MOD). This diving mode is also called over-bottom diving.
  B. Diving in blue-water presents a number of unique challenges including:
    1) Increased chances of vertigo;
    2) Exceeding depth limits;
    3) Exceeding allowable bottom times; and
    4) Increased breathing gas consumption due to the depth.
  C. Blue-water diving must be carefully planned and executed and approved by the LODO/SODO.

4.10.2 Equipment Requirements.
  A. All divers diving in blue-water conditions shall have a means to compensate for catastrophic loss of buoyancy (e.g., a lift bag, drysuit with BCD, or safety sausage) and a surface signaling device if un-tethered.
  B. No over-bottom dives shall be made unless some direct reference with the surface is maintained.

4.10.3 Training. At a minimum, blue-water dive training should include procedures for:
  A. Deploying and using any specialized harnesses or rigging that may be utilized; and
  B. Deploying a lift-bag via a line reel.

4.10.4 Emergency Procedures.
    A. Loss of positive buoyancy:
        1) Notify buddy diver of problem;
        2) Ditch weights or weight belt; or
        3) Deploy lift-bag using line-reel and pull self up the downline.
    B. Loss of spatial orientation or vertigo. Notify buddy diver of problem and with their assistance, terminate dive, and ascend to surface.

4.11 Overhead Obstruction Diving

4.11.1 General. This section covers any diving environment where the diver cannot easily reach the surface in the event of equipment failure or a compromised breathing supply due to an overhead physical obstruction. (This does not include ship husbandry dives.)

4.11.2 Equipment Requirements.
    A. Equipment used for scuba in an overhead environment is based on the concept of redundancy.
    B. In addition to standard scuba diving equipment, the following equipment is required when diving in an overhead environment:
        1) A diver-carried, independent reserve breathing gas supply with separate scuba regulator and sufficient gas volume to allow the diver to safely return to the surface;
        2) A slate and pencil; and
        3) Redundant underwater lights, knives, and line reels as deemed appropriate by the LODO/SODO.

4.11.3 Training and Proficiency.
    A. The requirement for overhead obstruction dive training will be left to the discretion of the LODO/SODO.
    B. Dive experience in lieu of training may be approved by the LODO/SODO.
    C. When diving of this type is not performed on a routine basis then 'work-up' dives shall be completed prior to the dive mission.

4.11.4 Diving Procedures.
    A. With this technique, a dive team shall be considered to be cavern diving if at any time during the dive they find themselves in a position where they cannot complete a direct, unobstructed vertical ascent to the surface because of rock formations.
    B. Overhead obstruction diving shall not be conducted at depths greater than 100 feet.
    C. Dive teams shall perform a safety drill prior to commencing cavern (overhead) diving operations that includes locating and rescuing a trapped diver.
    D. Each team within the cavern zone must utilize a continuous guideline appropriate for the environment leading to a point from which an uninterrupted vertical ascent to the surface may be made.
    E. Gas management must be appropriate for the planned dive.

4.12 Cold-Water Diving

4.12.1 General.
    A. Definition. Dives conducted in water temperatures colder than 50° F.

B. Due to the increased risks associated with cold water diving, such operations must be carefully planned and executed and pre-approved by the UDS.

C. Dives conducted in water temperatures colder than 50° F have the potential for regulator freeze-up.

4.12.2 Qualifications. Must be an authorized NOAA diver.

4.12.3 Required procedures. When conducting cold water dives, divers shall adhere to the following:

A. Refill SCUBA cylinders only at filling stations equipped with an efficient filtering and moisture removal system.

B. When preparing for a cold water dive, keep SCUBA cylinders and regulators in a place sheltered from the cold until just before starting the dive.

C. Open the SCUBA cylinder control valve for 1 or 2 seconds to make sure there are no water droplets or small ice crystals. Also check the inlet opening of the regulator.

D. For repetitive dives, take particular care to ensure the SCUBA regulator is completely dry before starting the second dive.

E. Avoid breathing from the regulator prior to immersion.

F. As much as possible, try to prevent water from entering inside the second stage during the dive.

G. Never operate the purge button unless underwater.

H. Use the purge button as little as possible. In any case, never hold it down for more than 2 or 3 consecutive seconds; pressing it for longer may cause ice to form.

I. Breathe normally in order to minimize the cooling effect produced by the higher air velocity during over breathing.

4.13   Snorkeling/Breath-Hold Diving

4.13.1 Scope. This section applies only to NOAA divers who conduct snorkeling as part of their official duties.

4.13.2 Qualifications. Must be an authorized NOAA diver.

4.13.3 Limits. Unless specifically authorized by the UDS, and upon review and approval of a dive plan and DEAP, snorkeling/breath-hold diving shall not be conducted:

A. At depths greater than 30 feet;

B. In areas with potential underwater entanglements;

C. In seas greater than 3-5 feet; or

D. In current greater than 0.5 knots.

4.13.4 Requirements.

A. Unless specifically authorized by the UDS, each snorkeler/breath-hold diver shall be equipped with:

1) Mask;
2) Fins;
3) Snorkel;
4) A flotation vest capable of providing positive buoyancy; and
5) Cutting device.

B. The UDS may also require a buddy snorkeler/breath-hold diver.

4.14   Diving Near Unexploded Ordinance

4.14.1 General. Interacting with unexploded ordinance is outside the scope of the NDP. NOAA divers shall not intentionally touch, move, bury, or in any other fashion interact with unexploded ordinance. This section only addresses the safety buffer zones NOAA divers shall maintain in the vicinity of unexploded ordinance and the reporting of the discovery of unexploded ordinance.

4.14.2 Safety Buffer Zones.
   A. Divers shall maintain a distance of at least 10 feet from unexploded ordinance with non-explosive projectiles (i.e., pistol, rifle, or machine gun ammunition); and
   B. Divers shall maintain a distance of at least 100 feet from unexploded ordinance with explosive projectiles or warheads (i.e., bombs, artillery shells, rockets, missiles, mines, or grenades).

4.14.3 Reporting. When found during a dive, divers should signal their dive buddies to the presence of unexploded ordinance and immediately proceed outside the appropriate buffer zone. Once on the surface, divers should notify the DM or LD of the location and type of unexploded ordinance present at the dive site.

4.15   Contaminated Water Diving

Diving in water contaminated with hazardous biological, chemical, or radioactive pollutants requires specialized training, equipment, and diving protocols; and is outside the scope of the NDP. Until such time that these elements are established, NOAA divers are prohibited from diving in contaminated water. Qualified contract divers should be hired to dive in these conditions.

4.16   Surface Supplied Diving Mode

Refer to Sections 6.6 and 7.5 NOAA Working Diving Standards and Safety Manual.

4.17   Hyperbaric Chamber Operations

Refer to Sections 6.11 and 7.2.6 NOAA Working Diving Standards and Safety Manual.

SECTION 5: DIVING EQUIPMENT

5.1 General Policy

5.1.1 Operation and Maintenance.
   A. All equipment (e.g., diver worn, dive support, air systems, hyperbaric chambers) shall be operated and maintained in accordance with the manufacturer's recommendations.
   B. All equipment shall be regularly examined by the person using it prior to diving.
   C. All equipment repair, test, calibration or maintenance service shall be recorded by means of a tagging or logging system, and shall include the date, nature of work performed, and the name or initials of the person or company performing the work.
   D. Equipment subjected to extreme usage under adverse conditions requires more frequent testing and maintenance.
   E. Any diving conducted using specialized equipment or procedures (e.g., drysuits, full face masks, tethered or line-tended SCUBA) shall be practiced on an annual basis to maintain proficiency. Failure to meet these minimum standards requires work-up dives to be conducted prior to making duty dives.
   F. All diving equipment shall be stored in a secure, properly ventilated space free of noxious fumes and corrosive elements.
   G. Diving units shall be afforded sufficient space to properly maintain and organize all diving equipment.
   H. An inventory of SEP issued diving equipment shall be conducted by each diver annually and the results submitted to the UDS.
   I. All equipment shall be free of corrosion and deterioration that may impede its intended use.

5.1.2 Oxygen Safety.
   A. Equipment used with gases containing over 40 percent by volume oxygen shall be designed for or adapted for oxygen service.
   B. Components (except umbilicals) exposed to gas mixtures containing over 40 percent by volume oxygen shall be cleaned of combustible materials before use.
   C. Oxygen systems over 125 psig and compressed air systems over 500 psig shall have slow-opening shut-off valves.

5.2 Support Equipment

5.2.1 Emergency Oxygen Kits.
   A. A positive-pressure ventilator and a bag-type manual resuscitator with transparent mask or equivalent capable of ventilating an unconscious victim shall be available at the dive location.
   B. Oxygen regulators must be capable of supplying oxygen to two individuals simultaneously, one via a demand/positive pressure regulator and the other via a non-return, free-flow mask.
   C. Sufficient quantity of oxygen to supply two divers for:
      1) The time required to transport them to a higher-level medical care facility; or
      2) 12 hours, whichever is less.
   D. The regulator and Elder valve positive pressure/demand regulators used to deliver oxygen shall be tested annually to ensure delivery pressure is within the manufacturer's specifications.

E. If an NDC issued regulator is determined to be out-of-specification, the NDC shall be notified and a replacement provided by NDC.

F. Oxygen kits shall be checked before every day of diving.

5.2.2   First Aid Kits.

A. A first aid kit appropriate for the dive location and approved by the NDP DMO shall be available at the dive location.

B. First aid kits shall have the minimum equipment and supplies as listed in the NOAA Small First Aid Kit contents list (See Appendix 9).

C. If the vessel/dive site has space available the NOAA Large First Aid Kit should be available.

5.2.3   Air Compressor Systems.

A. Air compressors shall be:
1) Maintained and operated in accordance with the manufacturer's recommended guidelines; and
2) Located in a space that is clean, free of flammable material, and sufficiently ventilated to prevent system overheating.

B. Air compressor intakes shall be clearly labeled and located away from areas containing exhaust or other contaminants.

C. Hearing protection shall be made available as necessary to comply with OSHA standards.

D. Air compressor relief valves shall be tested for proper operation annually.

E. The output of air compressor systems shall be tested for air purity every 6 months.

F. Non-oil lubricated compressors need not be tested for oil mist.

G. The test results shall be maintained both at the unit and NDC and easily accessible by all users upon request.

H. When possible, the test results should be posted near the compressor.

I. A log shall be maintained showing operation, repair, overhaul, filter maintenance, and temperature adjustment for each compressor.

J. A copy of the manufacturer's operators manual shall be readily available for reference and written operating procedures posted near the compressor.

K. All air system components (e.g., plumbing, valves, and gauges) shall be:
1) Properly rated for the working pressure of the system and labeled as to their functions; and
2) Properly secured to prevent injury.

L. Compressors used to supply air to the diver shall be equipped with a volume tank with a check valve on the inlet side, a pressure gauge, a relief valve, and a drain valve.

M. All SCUBA charging whips shall be:
1) Properly secured to prevent injury to personnel during cylinder filling operations; and
2) Visually inspected for damage or deterioration prior to each use.

N. All divers who fill scuba cylinders shall be properly trained in the specific procedures involved and the training shall be documented in the unit log.

O. Compressed gas cylinders. Shall:
1) Be designed, constructed and maintained in accordance with provisions of 29 CFR 1910.6 and 1910.169;
2) Be stored in a ventilated area and protected from excessive heat;
3) Be secured from falling;

4) Have shut-off valves recessed into the cylinder or protected by a cap, except when in use, interconnected, or when used for SCUBA diving;

5) All pressure gauges included in divers' air/gas breathing production and delivery systems shall be checked for accuracy on an annual basis and documented in a maintenance log; and

6) Be hydrostatically tested every 5 years if part of a bank of cylinders including those stamped with a star (★) in the codes.

5.2.4 Air Quality Standards. Breathing air for NOAA diving shall meet the following specifications as set forth in 29 CFR 1910.430 (b) (3).

NAVSEA 0910-LP-708-80000 USN Diving Manual, VOL 1, REV 4, 20 JAN1999, TBL 4-1	
Component	Maximum
Oxygen	20 - 22%
Carbon Dioxide	1000 PPM
Carbon Monoxide	20 PPM
Condensed Hydrocarbons	5 mg/m3
Total Hydrocarbons as Methane	25 PPM
Objectionable Odors	None

5.2.5 Breathing Gas Supply Hose Connectors. Shall:
A. Be made of corrosion-resistant materials;
B. Have a working pressure at least equal to the working pressure of the hose to which they are attached; and
C. Be resistant to accidental disengagement.

5.3   Open-Circuit SCUBA Diving Equipment

5.3.1 Minimum Equipment Requirements.
A. Unless approved by the LODO/SODO, each diver shall be configured consistent with the figures shown in Appendix 7.
B. At a minimum, all NOAA certified divers are required to use the following NOAA-issued dive equipment when conducting official duty dives, unless specifically approved by the LODO/SODO:
1) A primary breathing gas supply and regulator;
2) A diver-carried reserve breathing gas supply consisting of an independent reserve cylinder with a separate regulator (when required);
3) A redundant second stage regulator on the primary cylinder(s) for air sharing;
4) A pressure gauge for each independent cylinder, readable by the diver during the dive;
5) A face mask;
6) A snorkel;
7) A buoyancy compensation device;
8) A weight system capable of quick release;
9) A knife or other cutting device;

      10) A pair of swim fins;

      11) A timekeeping device;

      12) A depth gauge;

      13) Thermal protection appropriate for the conditions; and

      14) A whistle or other sound producing device.

  B. The valve of the reserve breathing gas supply shall be in the closed position prior to and during the dive to ensure the air supply will not unintentionally be depleted during the dive.

5.3.2 Regulators.

  A. Unless approved by the LODO/SODO, all SCUBA regulators other than those issued via the SEP shall be listed on the USN's Authorized for Navy Use list.

  B. SCUBA regulators shall be inspected, serviced and tested by a qualified technician prior to first use and every 12 months thereafter.

  C. Regulators shall consist of a primary first and second stage, an alternate second stage, and a submersible pressure gauge.

5.3.3 Buoyancy Compensator Devices.

  A. Buoyancy Compensator Devices (BCD) shall be worn on all dives utilizing SCUBA.

  B. BCDs shall enable the diver to achieve positive buoyancy during a dive, including at the surface, and be configured with a manually-activated inflation source, an oral inflation assembly, and an exhaust valve.

  C. The inflation assembly shall be serviced every 12 months from the date of issue.

  D. BCDs shall not be used as a lifting device in lieu of lift bags.

5.3.4 Gauges and Timekeeping Devices.

  A. Each independent cylinder used shall be equipped with a pressure gauge capable of being monitored by the diver during the dive.

  B. A timekeeping device shall be:

      1) Worn by each diver; and

      2) At the dive location for topside support.

5.3.5 SCUBA Cylinders. SCUBA cylinders shall be designed, constructed, and maintained in accordance with the applicable provisions of the Unfired Pressure Vessel Safety Orders.

5.3.6 Maintenance Requirements.

  A. SCUBA regulators, including first stages, second-stages and alternate second stage air sources, shall be serviced annually, unless more frequent service is deemed necessary.

  B. Depth gauges shall be tested:

      1) Every 6 months against a master reference gauge, with no deviation greater than +3.0/-0.0 fsw between any two equivalent gauges, and

      2) When there is a discrepancy greater than 2 percent of full scale between any two equivalent gauges.

  C Dive computers shall be tested:

      1) Annually against a master reference gauge, with no deviation greater than +3.0/-0.0 fsw between any two equivalent gauges, and

      2) When there is a discrepancy greater than 2 percent of full scale between any two equivalent gauges.

  D. Submersible pressure gauges shall be tested annually against a master reference gauge, with no deviation greater than +/- 10 percent of scale.

E. Buoyancy compensator device inflator assemblies shall be serviced annually in accordance with the manufacturer's recommended guidelines.

F. SCUBA cylinders must be hydrostatically tested in accordance with U.S. Department of Transportation standards and be internally and externally inspected by a qualified technician annually or when suspect.

G. SCUBA cylinder valves shall be functionally inspected at intervals not to exceed 12 months.

H. Standby diver tending line (without communication wires) shall be pull-tested annually to a minimum of 300 pounds.

I. Weight-harness systems with quick-release mechanisms shall be tested for proper function prior to each diving day.

5.3.7   Use of NOAA-Issued Diving Equipment Off-Duty.

A. General.

1) In order to maximize the safe conduct of diving operations, NOAA divers are required to regularly train to maintain a high level of proficiency through the performance of diving activities on a routine basis.

2) In recognition of the important benefits of regular dive training with a uniform set of diving equipment, NOAA divers may use NOAA-issued diving equipment on off-duty dives for the purpose of maintaining diving proficiency. Such training helps maintain familiarity with the controls and function of the equipment, develop muscle memory needed to react automatically during emergencies, and promote physical fitness.

B. Minimum Requirements.

1) NOAA divers shall be currently authorized to dive by the NDP in order to use SEP gear off-duty. Divers whose diving proficiency has lapsed may participate in the off-duty program for the purpose of obtaining reauthorization, with UDS approval.

2) Prior to using NOAA-issued diving equipment on off-duty dives, each diver must sign and comply with the NOAA Diver Agreement for the Use of SEP Gear Off-Duty and the SEP Off-Duty Liability Release available at www.ndc.noaa.gov. User Agreements and Liability Waivers are valid until December 31 of the year in which they are signed. Copies of these documents, with original signatures, will be maintained at the Diving Unit by the UDS.

3) Divers using SEP equipment on off-duty dives must complete two of the following skills during each dive:
   a) Ditch and don BCD;
   b) Weight belt removal / replacement;
   c) Disconnect / reconnect inflators (BCD/Dry Suit);
   d) Drysuit roll outs and venting;
   e) Buddy breathing;
   f) Air sharing;
   g) Deploy and use RASS;
   h) Recover unconscious diver from water;
   i) Mask removal, replace and clear;
   j) Maintain neutral buoyancy for 2 minutes;
   k) Control descent / ascent rate;
   l) Underwater communication (hand signals);
   m) Underwater navigation and orientation, and/or;
   n) Regulator recovery.

4) Completion of requirements in Section 5.3.7B3 above shall be noted on the SEP Off-Duty Proficiency Dive Skills Checklist and verified (in writing) by the diver's buddy following any off-duty dive with SEP gear. A copy of the signed checklist will be forwarded to the UDS and kept on file at the unit for a minimum of 30-days or forwarded electronically to ndp.diveplans@noaa.gov.

5) All off-duty dives using SEP equipment shall be logged as "Training/Proficiency" and "Non-Duty" using the NDP online dive logging system available at www.ndc.noaa.gov.

C. Eligibility.
   1) Only those NOAA divers in active status with the NDP and possessing SEP equipment are eligible to participate in the SEP off-duty diving program.
   2) Only NOAA employees and approved contractors are eligible to participate in the SEP.

D. Authority for accepting divers into the SEP off-duty diving program
   1) Authority for accepting divers into the SEP off-duty diving program rests with the UDS.
   2) The NOAA NDPM, LODO/SODO, or UDS may revoke approval for participation in this program for cause, at any time.

E. Limitations. Maximum depth and tasks authorized may be limited by the NDPM, LODO/SODO, or UDS based on review of the divers' resumes and dive logs.

F. Responsibilities.
   1) NOAA UDS.
      a) Reviews SEP NOAA Diver Agreement for the Use of SEP Gear Off-Duty and the SEP Off-Duty Liability Release for compliance with minimum requirements.
      b) Maintains records of NOAA Diver Agreement for the Use of SEP Gear Off-Duty and the SEP Off-Duty Liability Release for the duration of their validity and ensures SEP Off-Duty Proficiency Dive Skills Checklists are maintained for 30 days post-dive or forwarded electronically to ndp.diveplans@noaa.gov.
      c) Monitors adherence to standards outlined in the NOAA Diver Agreement for the Use of SEP Gear Off-Duty and suspends SEP off-duty use if violations are detected.
   2) NOAA LODO/SODO.
      a) Reviews and grants approval for SEP off-duty equipment use for divers whose proficiency has lapsed by more than 6 months.
      b) Monitors adherence to standards outlined in the NOAA Diver Agreement for the Use of SEP Gear Off-Duty and suspends SEP off-duty use if violations are detected.
   3) NOAA NDPM. Monitors adherence to standards outlined in the NOAA Diver Agreement for the Use of SEP Gear Off-Duty and suspends SEP off-duty use if violations are detected.

5.4   Tethered SCUBA Diving Equipment

5.4.1 Servicing and Testing. The following annual servicing and testing is required for all tethered SCUBA diving systems:
A. All full-face masks used for tethered SCUBA diving must be serviced by a certified repair technician annually.
B. The entire communication/strength tether, including the seizing of the "D" ring on the tether, must be visually inspected annually.

5.4.2 Documentation. Results of annual servicing and inspection shall be noted on the annual diving unit safety assessment checklist.

5.5   Surface Supplied Diving Equipment

Refer to Section 7.5 NOAA Working Diving Standards and Safety Manual.

5.6   Hyperbaric Chamber Equipment and Systems

Refer to Section 7.2.6 NOAA Working Diving Standards and Safety Manual.

SECTION 6: MEDICAL STANDARDS

6.1   Medical Standards and Procedures for NOAA Diving

6.1.1. General.
   A. The information contained within this Manual does not address all medical standards and procedures for diving under the auspices of NOAA.
   B. The NOAA Diving Medical Standards and Procedures Manual (NDMSPM), provides uniform criteria and interpretation of physical qualification for diving duties and should be referred to for specific information on medical standards for NOAA diving.
   C. The NDMSPM, which is based on standards from current dive medicine practice within a variety of government and civilian organizations, as well as experts in dive medicine, can be viewed and downloaded from the NDC website at www.ndc.noaa.gov.

6.1.2   Purpose. The NDMSPM was developed to ensure individuals diving under the auspices of NOAA are:
   A. Free of contagious diseases or medical conditions likely to endanger the health or safety of themselves or other personnel in the course of their diving duties;
   B. Medically capable of performing duties without significant aggravation of existing physical defects or medical conditions that compromise diver safety or performance;
   C. Free of medical conditions or physical defects that would likely result in termination from the NDP for medical unfitness.
   D. Medically fit to perform the duties of a NOAA diver.

6.1.3   Scope.
   A. The Standards contained in the NDMSPM apply to all personnel who are authorized to dive under the NDP.
   B. NOAA reserves the right to deny diving privileges to anyone deemed unfit to dive by the NDMRB.
   C. Medical Clearance Authority.
      1) Authority for medical clearance for diving resides with NOAA.
      2) Objective data and opinions from physicians and other medical practitioners will be reviewed as input for decisions on NOAA fitness to dive; however, the ultimate decision authority on fitness to dive rests with the NDP DMO.

6.2   Medical Examinations

6.2.1   General Information.
   A. All medical examinations must be conducted by a MD, DO, NP, or PA licensed in the United States.
   B. NOAA Forms (NF) 56-69, NDP Report of Medical History, and NF 56-70, NDP Report of Physical Examination Form, must be completed, signed and dated by the examiner at the time the physical examination is performed.

6.2.2   Examination Types, Timing and Frequency of Medical Examinations.
   A. Examination types
      1) An initial medical examination is required of all new applicants for dive certification as well as for all NOAA divers whose certification has lapsed for more than 2 years.

2) Periodic medical examinations are required of all active NOAA divers.
3) The Annual Medical Status Report shall be completed by all divers and is due to the NDP DMO in the anniversary month of divers' current physical exams. An Annual Medical Status Report is not required the year a diver is due to complete a periodic medical exam.

B. Examination validity. The following standards apply to all NOAA dive physicals.

Age (in years) at time of last physical	Time between physicals
18-47	5 years
48	4 years
49	3 years
50-59	2 years
60+	1 year

C. Physical examination requirements (See NDMSPM).

6.2.3 Reciprocity Divers.
A. The NDCSB may authorize divers to participate in NOAA diving operations based on certification by external agencies with whom NOAA has written reciprocity agreements.
B. No review of medical records by the NDP is routinely required for these individuals. However, individuals for whom a specific independent reason exists to believe they may not be fit to dive, may be asked to provide additional medical information and justification prior to allowing the individual to dive with NOAA.

6.2.4. Observer Divers. Observer Diver candidates shall submit Form NF 56-76, NDP Observer Diver Medical History, signed by an MD, DO, NP, or PA licensed in the United States, to the NDP DMO for review and approval.

6.2.5 Recordkeeping.
A. All diver physical examinations and medical information are protected under the Privacy Act of 1974, 5 U.S.C. § 552a, Public Law No. 93-579, (December 31, 1974).
B. The NDC shall maintain medical records for each NOAA Diver certified in a secure location.
C. All medically-related documents shall be sent to the attention of the NDP DMO. All documents so submitted shall be:
1) Treated as confidential as required by federal privacy laws; and
2) Retained in accordance with applicable federal statutes.
D. Availability of Records.
1) Medical records shall only be released upon written authorization of the diver or former diver.
2) Records and documents required by this standard shall be retained as outlined in Section 12.1.4 of this Manual.

6.3 Reporting Changes in Medical Condition

6.3.1 Requirements.
  A. Divers are responsible for immediately reporting information concerning changes to their medical qualifications for diving duty.
  B. Any new medical condition <u>other than minor acute episodic illness</u> since completion of the diver's last history and/or physical must be reported immediately to the UDS and then followed up in writing to the NDP DMO. This includes any surgery, no matter how complex, hospitalizations, fractures, or other injuries to bone or joint.
  C. Changes in medical condition must be reported on an annual basis on NOAA Form 56-77, NDP Annual Medical Status Report.

6.3.2 Consequences of Non-Disclosure.
  A. Any evidence of either nondisclosure or falsification of medical information shall result in suspension of diving certification pending investigation by the NDCSB.
  B. If the investigation reveals that the diver intentionally withheld or falsified information, his/her diving certification may be summarily terminated.

6.4 Lapsed Dive Physicals

6.4.1 Expiration of Diving Physicals.
  A. NOAA Diver physical exams expire 12, 24, 36, 48, or 60 months from the date the physical exam was performed based on the age of the diver (Section 6.2.2).
  B. If a diver's physical has lapsed for less than 24 months, they must submit a periodic physical with all required tests to the NDP DMO for assessment of fitness to dive.
  C. If a diver's physical has lapsed for 24 months or longer, they shall be required to submit an initial physical with all required tests. The chest x-ray shall only be required at the discretion of the NDP DMO.

6.4.2 Annual Medical Status Report. Failure to submit an Annual Medical Status Report by the end of the month which appears in the date box of the current physical exam shall result in temporary suspension of diving privileges until such time as the form is submitted and reviewed.

6.5 Funding for NOAA Diving Physical Examinations

6.5.1 General.
  A. In order to maximize the safe conduct of diving operations, NOAA divers are required to meet initial and periodic medical and fitness standards for diving.
  B. In recognition of the important benefits of being medically and physically fit to dive, NOAA Line and Staff Offices (LO/SO) are authorized to use government funds to cover costs associated with obtaining physical examinations for diving purposes.
  C. In lieu of using government funds to pay for diving physical examinations, LO/SO may choose to require employees to obtain the examinations via their personal health insurance programs. In such cases, LO/SO may reimburse NOAA employees for costs not covered by their personal health insurance programs.

6.5.2   Eligibility.
   A. In order to use government funds for the purpose of obtaining diving physical examinations, individuals must be NOAA employees, currently certified as NOAA divers, or eligible to obtain NOAA diving certification, either initially or in a recertification program.
   B. Use of government funds to pay for diving physical examinations is limited to the following classifications of NOAA federal employees: NOAA Corps Officers, and Commerce Alternate Pay System, Wage Grade, and Wage Marine employees.

6.5.3   Authority for Approving Government Funding of NOAA Diving Physicals Exams. Final authority to expend government funds for the purpose of obtaining diving physical examinations rests with the appropriate LO/SO unit, program, or ship official.

6.5.4   Responsibilities.
   A. NOAA Diver or Diver Candidate. Discusses funding options with appropriate UDS and NOAA funding manager.
   B. NOAA Unit Diving Supervisor
      1) Participates in discussion on funding options with diver, or diver candidate, and NOAA funding manager.
      2) Provides input on funding option to appropriate funding manager.
   C. NOAA Funding Manager
      1) Participates in discussion on funding options with diver, or diver candidate, and UDS.
      2) Notifies diver, or diver candidate, and UDS of decision.

SECTION 7: NITROX DIVING

7.1 General

The following guidelines address the use of Nitrox by scientific divers under NOAA auspices. For these standards, Nitrox is defined as any gas mixture being comprised of an oxygen concentration higher than 22 percent by volume.

7.2 Prerequisites

Only certified Scientific Divers (Section 3.1) diving under NOAA auspices or under the authority of a recognized reciprocity organization are eligible for authorization to use Nitrox.

7.3 Requirements for Authorization to Use Nitrox

7.3.1 Final Approval.
   A. Submission of documents and successful completion of a written examination does not automatically result in authorization to use Nitrox.
   B. The applicant must demonstrate sufficient skills and proficiency to the NDPM or his/her designee.

7.3.2 Minimum Activity to Maintain Authorization.
   A. The diver should log at least one Nitrox dive per year.
   B. Failure to meet the minimum activity level may be cause for restriction or revocation of Nitrox authorization.

7.4 Nitrox Training Requirements

7.4.1 General. The minimum academic and practical instruction listed in this section must be mastered in order to receive a Nitrox Certification from NOAA.

7.4.2 Classroom Instruction.
   A. Topics should include, but are not limited to:
      1) Physical gas laws pertaining to Nitrox, partial pressure calculations and limits, and equivalent air depth (EAD) concept and calculations;
      2) Oxygen physiology and oxygen toxicity and calculation of oxygen exposure and MOD;
      3) Determination of decompression schedules (both by EAD method using approved air dive tables, and using approved Nitrox dive tables);
      4) Dive planning and emergency procedures;
      5) Gas analysis;
      6) Personnel requirements; and
      7) Equipment marking and maintenance requirements.
   B. The NDCSB may choose to limit standard Nitrox diver training to procedures applicable to diving, and reserve training such as Nitrox production methods, and oxygen cleaning.

7.4.3   Practical Training.
    A. The practical training portion will consist of the following:
        1) Oxygen analysis and logging of Nitrox gases;
        2) Determination of MOD, oxygen partial pressure exposure, and oxygen toxicity time limits, for various Nitrox gases at various depths; and
        3) Determination of nitrogen-based dive limits status by EAD method using air dive tables, and/or using Nitrox dive tables, as approved by the NDCSB.
    B. Nitrox dive computer use may be included (Section 4.5.5).

7.4.4   Written Examination. Before authorization, the trainee shall successfully pass a written examination demonstrating knowledge of at least the following:
    A. Function, care, use, and maintenance of equipment cleaned for Nitrox use;
    B. Physical and physiological considerations of Nitrox diving;
    C. Diving standards and procedures as related to Nitrox diving;
    D. Given the proper information, calculation of:
        1) Equivalent air depth (EAD) for a given FO_2 and actual depth
        2) PO_2 exposure for a given FO_2 and depth
        3) Appropriate Nitrox gas for a given PO_2 exposure limit, and planned depth and time;
        4) MOD for a given gas blend and PO_2 exposure limits;
    E. Dive table selection and usage;
    F. Nitrox production methods and considerations;
    G. Oxygen analysis; and
    H. Nitrox operational guidelines and dive planning.

7.4.5   Open-Water Dives.
    A. A minimum of two supervised open-water dives is required prior to using Nitrox.
    B. If the MOD for the gas being used can be easily exceeded at the training location, direct, in-water supervision is required.

7.5   Dive Personnel Requirements

7.5.1   Scientific Diver.
    A. NOAA Scientific Divers who have completed the requirements of Section 7.4 may be authorized by the NDPM to use Nitrox.
    B. Depth authorization to use Nitrox should be the same as that specified in the diver's authorization, as described in Section 3.3 or equivalent to the depth rating of advanced certifications (i.e. advanced EANx diver)

7.5.2   Divemaster / Lead Diver.
    A. On any dive during which Nitrox will be used by any team member, the DM/LD should be authorized to use Nitrox, and hold appropriate authorizations required for the dive, as specified in this Manual.
    B. DM/LD authorization for Nitrox dives by the UDS (or designee) should occur as part of the dive project approval process.
    C. In addition to responsibilities listed in Section 2.6, the DM/LD shall:
        1) As part of the dive planning process, verify that all divers using Nitrox on a dive are properly qualified and authorized.
        2) As part of the pre-dive procedures, confirm with each diver the oxygen percentage of the gas the diver is using, and establish dive team maximum depth

and time limits, according to the shortest time limit or shallowest depth limit among the team members.

3) Reduce the maximum allowable PO_2 exposure limit for the dive team if on-site conditions so indicate.

7.6 Nitrox Diving Parameters

7.6.1 Oxygen Exposure Limits.
   A. The inspired oxygen partial pressure experienced at depth should not exceed 1.6 ATA. All dives performed using Nitrox breathing gases should comply with the current NOAA Diving Manual "Oxygen Partial Pressure Limits for 'Normal' Exposures."
   B. The maximum allowable exposure limit should be reduced in cases where cold or strenuous dive conditions, or extended exposure times are expected. The UDS should consider this in the review of any dive plan application which proposes to use Nitrox.

7.6.2 Bottom Time Limits.
   A. Maximum bottom time should be based on the depth of the dive and the Nitrox gas being used.
   B. Bottom time for a single dive should not exceed the NOAA maximum allowable "Single Exposure Limit" for a given oxygen partial pressure, as listed in the most recent edition of the NOAA Diving Manual.

7.6.3 Dive Tables and Gases.
   A. A set of NDCSB-approved Nitrox dive tables shall be available at the dive site.
   B. When using the EAD method, dives should be conducted using air dive tables approved by the NDCSB.
   C. If Nitrox is used to increase the safety margin of air-based dive tables, the MOD, oxygen exposure and time limits for Nitrox gases being dived shall not be exceeded.
   D. Nitrox breathing gases used while performing in-water decompression, or for bail-out purposes, should contain the same or greater oxygen content as that being used during the dive, within the confines of depth limitations and oxygen partial pressure limits set forth in Section 7.6.1 of this Manual.

7.6.4 Nitrox Dive Computers.
   A. Any commercially available Nitrox dive computer may be used for no-decompression diving by completing a Dive Computer User Agreement, available from the NDC website.
   B. Dive computers for decompression dives must be approved by the NDCSB.
   C. Prior to using a Nitrox dive computer, users shall demonstrate, to the satisfaction of the UDS or designee, a clear understanding of the display, operations, and manipulation of the unit being used.
   D. Dive computers capable of PO_2 limit and FO_2 adjustment should be checked by the diver prior to the start each dive to assure compatibility with the gas being used.

7.6.5 Repetitive Diving.
   A. Repetitive dives using Nitrox gases should be performed in compliance with procedures required of the specific dive tables used or as prescribed by the manufacturer of a Nitrox diving computer.

B. When determining residual nitrogen times using EAD calculations, the time shall be based on the Nitrox gas mixture to be used on the repetitive dive, and not that from the previous dive.

C. The total cumulative exposure for PO_2 shall remain within Repetitive Excursion (REPEX) limits as provided in the NOAA Diving Manual.

7.6.6 Oxygen Parameters.

A. Authorized Nitrox Gases. Gases meeting the criteria outlined in this section may be used for Nitrox diving operations.

B. Purity. Oxygen used for Nitrox-breathing gas shall meet the purity levels for "Medical Grade" (U.S.P.), Technical Diving Grade, or "Aviator Grade" standards.

C. In addition to the Air Quality Guidelines (Section 5.2.4), the following standard shall be met for breathing air that is either: placed in contact with oxygen concentrations greater than 40 percent or used in Nitrox production by the partial pressure blending method with gases containing greater than 40 percent oxygen as the enriching agent.

ANALYTE	Membrane Systems	Partial Pressure Systems
Oxygen	20 - 22	20 - 22
Carbon Dioxide (ppmv)	1000	1000
Carbon Monoxide (ppmv)	20	10
Total Gaseous Hydrocarbons including Methane (ppmv)	25	25
Oil Mist and Particulate (mg/m$_3$)	5	5
Oil Mist (mg/m$_3$)	N/A	0.1
Particulate (mg/m$_3$)	N/A	0.1
Odor (Objectionable)	None	None
Methane (ppmv)	N/A	N/A

7.6.7 Diver Responsibility for Gas Analysis.

A. Individuals responsible for producing and/or analyzing Nitrox gases shall be trained and experienced in all aspects of the technique.

B. In situations where NOAA owns or operates the compressors, only those trained individuals approved by the UDS shall be responsible for blending Nitrox gases.

C. It is the responsibility of the UDS to approve the specific Nitrox production method used.

D. Prior to the dive, it is the responsibility of each diver to analyze the oxygen content of their SCUBA cylinder and acknowledge in writing the following information for each cylinder:
1) FO_2;
2) MOD;
3) Cylinder pressure;
4) Date of analysis; and
5) User's name.

E. Individual dive log reporting forms should report FO_2 of Nitrox used, if different than 21 percent.

7.7   Nitrox Diving Equipment

7.7.1   General.
   A. All designated equipment and stated requirements regarding SCUBA equipment required in this Manual should apply to Nitrox SCUBA operations.
   B. Additional minimal equipment necessary for Nitrox diving operations includes labeled SCUBA cylinders and oxygen analyzers.

7.7.2   Oxygen Cleaning and Maintenance Requirements.
   A. All equipment exposed to oxygen concentrations greater than 40 percent by volume at pressures above 200 psi, shall be cleaned and maintained for oxygen clean service.
   B. Oxygen systems over 125 psig shall have slow-opening shut-off valves.

7.7.3   SCUBA Cylinder Identification.
   A. Cylinders shall be marked "NITROX," "EANx," or "Enriched Air."
   B. Nitrox identification color-coding should include a 4-inch wide green band around the cylinder. If the cylinder is not yellow, the green band should be bordered above and below by a 1-inch yellow band.
   C. The alternate marking of a yellow cylinder by painting the cylinder crown green and printing the word "NITROX" parallel to the length of the cylinder in 2-inch green letters is acceptable.
   D. Other markings, which identify the cylinder as containing gases other than air, may be used with the approval of the NDCSB.
   E. A contents label should be affixed, to include the current FO_2, date of analysis, name or initials of the person who analyzed the gas, and MOD.
   F. The cylinder should be labeled to indicate whether the cylinder is prepared for gases containing greater than 40 percent oxygen.
   G. SCUBA cylinders specifically designated for use with Nitrox breathing gases should only be filled with appropriate Nitrox gases or oxygen compatible air and should be analyzed and labeled appropriately.

7.7.4   Other Support Equipment.
   A. All Nitrox mixtures shall be analyzed using an oxygen analyzer capable of reading a scale of 0 to 100 percent oxygen, within 1 percent accuracy.
   B. All diver and support equipment should be suitable for the fraction of oxygen (FO_2) being used.

7.7.5   Nitrox Mixing Equipment and Procedures. All equipment and procedures used for the mixing of Nitrox breathing gases shall comply with standards outlined in the latest version of the NOAA Diving Manual.

SECTION 8: STAGED DECOMPRESSION SCUBA DIVING

8.1 Introduction and Scope

This standard specifies minimum requirements for conducting decompression diving operations using open circuit SCUBA to ensure a minimum level of safety. It applies to all personnel engaged in diving activities under the auspices of the NOAA Diving Program. Exceptions to this standard will be considered by the NDCSB on a case-by-case basis and may be approved if such exceptions are deemed as safe as or safer than those listed in this document.

8.2 Qualifications

8.2.1 Certification and Authorization.
   A. Divers must be trained and certified by the NDP or another NOAA-approved certification agency (i.e., International Association of Nitrox and Technical Diving, NAUI) for the equipment, depth, and gas mixture of the proposed dive plan.
   B. Divers must be currently authorized to dive by the NDP or another NOAA-approved diving program

8.2.2 Proficiency Requirements.
   A. In order to participate in decompression diving operations, divers must have performed a minimum of 12 dives in the last 6 months.
   B. Divers must also have completed one (1) dive within the previous 30-day period in the minimum equipment configuration to be used on the project.

8.3 Equipment

8.3.1 General.
   A. Valve and regulator systems for primary (bottom) gas supplies shall be configured with a minimum of 2 regulators (consisting of a first and second stage) each with its own on/off valve that allows continuous gas delivery in the event of failure of any one component of the regulator/valve system.
   B. Minimum diver-worn equipment required:
      1) Buoyancy control device;
      2) Depth gauge;
      3) Dive timing devices;
      4) Decompression tables;
      5) Lift bag and line reel;
      6) Cutting device;
      7) Signaling device; and
      8) Slate and pencil.

8.3.2 SCUBA Cylinders.
   A. For SCUBA cylinders used on dives >130 fsw it is recommended that they be outfitted with DIN valves.
   B. If using a single cylinder, an auxiliary gas supply with adequate volume to reach the next gas supply is required.

C. Dual cylinders should be connected with a dual manifold with isolation valves and be adjusted on the backpack/harness assembly so that divers can open/close each cylinder and manifold valve.

D. SCUBA cylinders used for decompression shall be color-coded and labeled in accordance with the following standards:

Gas	Cylinder Color	Labeling
Air	Any color	None
Oxygen	White or Green	"Oxygen" stenciled in 3-inch high color-contrasting letters
Nitrox	Yellow	4-inch green band with "NITROX" or "Enriched Air" stenciled in 2-inch high letters
	Other	Non-yellow cylinders have an additional 1-inch yellow band above and below the green label
Trimix	Any color	"Trimix" stenciled in 3-inch high color-contrasting letters
Heliox	Any color	"Heliox" stenciled in 3-inch high color-contrasting letters

E. The MOD, based on a maximum PO_2 of 1.6 ATA, of each breathing gas/cylinder (other than air) must be displayed in 3-inch high letters along the side of the cylinder, both facing inward towards the diver and outwards so other divers can identify the cylinder contents.

8.3.3 SCUBA Regulators.
A. Dual cylinders shall be outfitted with redundant SCUBA regulators.
B. The primary supply regulator shall be configured with a hose of adequate length to facilitate effective emergency gas sharing in the intended environment.
C. Regulators used with oxygen supplies shall be secured in a way (e.g., pouch or bungee) that reduces the possibility of inadvertent use at depths that would result in a hyperoxic exposure.

8.3.4 Buoyancy Control.
A. Divers shall have the capability to achieve positive buoyancy at all depths.
B. Acceptable means of buoyancy control include:
1) Dual-bladder buoyancy compensators with separate inflator hoses, or
2) Single-bladder buoyancy compensators with a variable-volume drysuit, each with separate inflator hoses.
C. When wearing dual cylinders, top and bottom dump valves shall be provided for the primary BCD bladder, with a top dump valve standard for the redundant backup bladder. Each bladder must be capable of achieving positive buoyancy at all depths and be outfitted with an over pressurization relief valve.

8.3.5 Depth and Cylinder Pressure Gauges.
A. Each diver shall have a redundant means of monitoring depth. At least one (1) of the devices shall be capable of recording the maximum depth obtained during dives for display once on the surface.
B. Each gas supply will have its own dedicated submersible pressure gauge.

8.3.6 Dive Timing Devices.
A. Each diver shall have a redundant means of tracking dive time.
B. Examples of acceptable devices include dive computers, bottom timers, and watches.

8.3.7   Signaling Devices.
  A. Unless approved by the DM or LD, each diver shall carry the following surface signaling devices:
      1) SMB (surface marker buoy or lift bag);
      2) Signal mirror; and
      3) Whistles or other audible signaling devices.
  B. If dives are conducted within 2 hours of sunset, each diver must also carry a flashlight and/or strobe light.
  C. If diving in an area in which the divers may become significantly separated from surface support vessels, then each diver should also carry a diver radio, Personal Locator Beacon (PLB) or a Personal Emergency Position-Indicating Radio Beacon (PEPIRB).

8.3.8   Lift Bag and Line Reel.
  A. Each diver shall carry a lift bag (minimum of 50 pounds (22.7 Kg) buoyancy) and a line reel with line equal to 1.5 times the maximum depth anticipated during a dive.
  B. Redundant lift bags and line reels may be required at the discretion of the on-site DM or LD.

8.3.9   Support Boats.
  A. There must be a means of extracting an unconscious victim from the water in a timely manner at all times during decompression dive operations.
  B. In addition to any NOAA small boat requirements, each boat shall carry an oxygen resuscitator capable of ventilating an unconscious victim and a minimum of one (1) spare cylinder of each type of decompression gas used on the dive.

8.3.10 Hyperbaric Chamber.
  A. A hyperbaric chamber shall be accessible within 2 hours of the dive site.
  B. A plan shall be prepared and verified to transport an injured diver to a hyperbaric chamber within the required time frame.
  C. Only ASME, ABS, or equivalent certifying authority – including current Pressure Vessel for Human Occupancy – hyperbaric chambers may be used.

8.4   Breathing Gases and Gas Management

8.4.1   General.
  A. All gases used for diving must be of breathing quality (e.g., medical or aviator grade).
  B. All breathing mixtures to be used for diving shall be analyzed for oxygen content using an oxygen analyzer. Gases must test within acceptable parameters as specified in the dive tables or computers used.
  C. It is the responsibility of each diver to confirm and verify in writing the oxygen content of his/her SCUBA cylinder(s) prior to commencing diving and acknowledge the following:
      1) PO_2 cut off depth (Maximum Operating Depth (MOD)) and appropriate gas mixture(s) to be used for each phase of the dive;
      2) Planned maximum depth and bottom time for the dive; and
      3) Availability of adequate volumes of gas as determined by review of cylinder pressures.

D. When physiologically appropriate, and approved by the NDCSB, Nitrox and/or 100 percent oxygen may be substituted for compressed air during ascent and/or decompression stops.

E. Each diver is responsible for calculating and carrying the required volume of breathing gases needed for each phase of the dive including the contingency of next deeper depth and bottom time, plus reserves. Each diver shall maintain a reserve volume capable of allowing both divers in a dive team to ascend safely and comfortably to a depth at which they may switch to a supplemental decompression gas. If no supplemental cylinders are utilized, then each diver should reserve sufficient gas volume to allow both divers to ascend to the surface, including any required decompression stops.

8.4.2 Oxygen.

A. Breathing gases used while performing in-water decompression shall contain the same or greater oxygen content as that used during the bottom phase of the dive. Interruption of high oxygen partial pressure decompression may be conducted with appropriate back gas mixtures or air as approved in the dive plan.

B. All gas systems, components, and storage containers used with oxygen mixtures above 40 percent by volume, must be formally cleaned in accordance with the most recent edition of the NOAA Diving Manual and this Manual.

C. Oxygen used for diving or Nitrox preparation or decompression shall meet or exceed the purity levels for Medical (U.S.P.), Technical Diving Grade, or Aviator Grade oxygen.

8.4.3 Air. Compressed air used with oxygen concentrations greater than 40 percent or when used in the preparation of Nitrox breathing mixtures with greater than 40 percent oxygen as the enriching agent, shall meet or exceed standards outlined in Section 7.6.6 of this manual.

8.5 Manning Requirements

8.5.1 Minimum Diving Positions and Capabilities.

A. Bottom divers.
   1) A minimum of two (2) divers, functioning as a buddy team, are required for all decompression SCUBA diving operations.
   2) Divers shall remain in sufficient proximity to each other at all times during the dive so they can render immediate assistance to each other if necessary.

B. Standby and Safety Divers
   1) A minimum of two (2) surface-based standby divers, functioning as a buddy team, are required for all decompression SCUBA diving operations involving less than three (3) bottom divers.
   2) Standby divers shall be similarly equipped and configured as the bottom divers and ready to enter the water within 2 minutes of notification.
   3) For decompression SCUBA diving operations involving three (3) or more bottom divers, the DM may choose to utilize an on-bottom safety diver in lieu of surface-based standby divers based on an operational risk assessment of the operation. If the decision is to use on-bottom safety diver(s), then at least one (1) of the bottom safety divers must have no responsibilities other than to monitor and assist the other bottom divers in an emergency.

C. Support Divers. Two (2) support divers to support the bottom divers during the decompression phase of the dive occurring shallower than 130 fsw may be required by the onsite DM or LD.

8.5.2   Minimum Topside Support.
A. Divemaster/Lead Diver:
  1) Must remain at the surface during diving operations; and
  2) Must be approved by the NDCSB.
B. Vessel/boat captain:
  1) Must remain on the vessel/boat during diving operations; and
  2) Must concur with the DM/LD on the commencement of diving operations and can terminate diving due to weather, vessel-related operational problems, or any other factors that may jeopardize the safety of the operation.

8.6   Operational Requirements

8.6.1   Dive Planning.
A. Dive condition limits: The DM and the Vessel Captain shall assess current and predicted weather conditions, sea state, and current speed and direction; and decide whether or not diving can be safely initiated.
B. Diver Communications.
  1) Bottom divers must be able to signal topside personnel at all times during the dive.
  2) Signaling protocols must be established that allow the differentiation between routine and emergency situations.

8.6.2   Decompression Calculation.
A. All decompression tables must be approved by the NDCSB.
B. The use of dive computers and/or decompression table generating computer programs must be approved by the NDCSB.
C. Each diver must carry a set of decompression dive tables. Additionally, one over and one under contingency time schedule will be carried by each bottom diver.

8.6.3   Maximum Depth and Bottom Time.
A. The maximum depth for decompression diving using open circuit SCUBA equipment shall be such that the PN_2 does not exceed 4 ATA.
B. The MOD for a given breathing mixture shall not exceed an oxygen partial pressure of 1.6 ATA.
C. Combined bottom and decompression times will not exceed the maximum allowable exposure time for a given partial pressure of oxygen as listed in the latest edition of the NOAA Diving Manual.
D. Repetitive dives may be approved by the DM/LD if appropriate and approved diving tables and procedures are available.

8.6.4   Diving Procedures.
A. Deployment.
  1) The procedures involved with descending to the bottom (e.g., use of down-line versus "free dropping") will be determined by the DM/LD.

    2) If the members of the bottom team get separated during descent and cannot locate each other within 5 minutes of reaching the bottom, both divers will terminate the dive and begin ascent/decompression.

    3) No additional dives may be started until all members of the previous dive team have completed their in-water decompression and have been on the surface for a minimum of 30 minutes.

B. On-bottom. The decision to remove and stage decompression cylinders once on the bottom must be approved by the DM/LD.

C. Ascent. The procedures involved with ascending to the surface (e.g., use of ascent-line versus "drift decompression") will be determined by the DM/LD.

8.6.5   Contingency Protocols.

A. The following contingency protocols shall be established, practiced, and reviewed by all participants prior to commencement of diving:

    1) Out of Gas;

       a) Bottom mix failure.

       b) Decompression staged gases failure.

    2) Aborted dive procedures;

    3) Omitted decompression;

    4) Lost bottom divers;

       a) Separation during deployment.

       b) Unable to reach down-line.

       c) Unable to locate ascent-line.

       d) Separated on dive site.

       e) Separated or swept off dive site.

       f) Entanglement on bottom.

       g) Buoy/down-line breakaway.

    5) Central Nervous System (CNS) Oxygen Toxicity;

    6) Change in environmental conditions during dive;

       a) Increase in current;

       b) Increase in surface waves and/or swells;

       c) Change in water temperature; and

       d) Reduction of surface visibility (especially fog).

B. Post-dive incident review:

    1) Following the actual occurrence of any of the above scenarios, a post-dive "stand down" will be initiated to thoroughly review the incident. After review of the incident, mitigation protocols will be established to prevent a reoccurrence and the "stand down" may be lifted by the DM/LD.

    2) If deemed a "near-miss" an incident report will be written and submitted in accordance with NOAA Diving Program and SECO requirements.

8.7   Dive Plan

8.7.1   General.

A. Diving projects involving the use of equipment other than open circuit design, use of gas mixtures other than air or Nitrox, or bottom times outside the no-decompression limits must be approved by the NDCSB before diving activities begin.

B. In order to evaluate the proposed diving activities, a detailed dive plan must be submitted to the NDCSB for review a minimum of 30 days prior to the commencement of diving operations.

8.7.2 Submission and Review Requirements. The dive plan shall include, but not be limited to, the following elements:
A. Overview of the operations;
B. Goals, objectives, and tasks to be accomplished;
C. Description and location of dive site;
D. Names, affiliations, roles/responsibilities, and qualifications of all participants;
E. Schedule of operations;
F. Description of equipment and facilities;
G. Logistical arrangements and considerations;
H. Normal and emergency diving procedures;
I. Diving Emergency Assistance Plan; and
J. Supporting documents, permits, and forms.

SECTION 9: MIXED GAS DIVING

9.1 General

Mixed gas diving is defined as dives conducted while breathing gas mixes containing proportions greater than 1 percent by volume of an inert gas other than nitrogen.

9.2 Minimum Experience and Training Requirements

9.2.1 Prerequisites.
    A. Nitrox certification and authorization per Section 7.4.
    B. If the intended use entails required decompression stops, divers shall be previously certified and authorized in decompression diving per Section 8.2.
    C. Divers shall demonstrate to the satisfaction of the NDCSB, sufficient skills, knowledge, and attitude appropriate for training in the safe use of mixed gases.

9.2.2 Classroom Training. Shall include, but not be limited to:
    A. Review of topics and issues previously outlined in Nitrox and staged decompression diving training as pertinent to the planned operations.
    B. The use of helium or other inert gases, and the use of multiple decompression gases.
    C. Equipment configurations and modifications.
    D. Mixed gas decompression planning.
    E. Gas management planning.
    F. Thermal considerations.
    G. Equivalent Narcotic Depth (END) determination.
    H. Mission planning and logistics.
    I. Emergency procedures.
    J. Mixed gas mixing methods.
    K. Methods of gas handling and cylinder filling.
    L. Oxygen exposure management.
    M. Gas analysis.
    N. Mixed gas physics and physiology.

9.2.3 Practical Training. Shall include, but not be limited to:
    A. Confined water session(s) in which divers demonstrate proficiency in required skills and techniques for proposed diving operations.
    B. A minimum of six (6) open water training dives.
    C. At least one (1) initial dive shall be in 130 fsw or less to practice equipment handling and emergency procedures.
    D. Subsequent dives will gradually increase in depth, with a majority of the training dives being conducted between 130 fsw and the planned operational depth.
    E. Planned operational depth for initial training dives shall not exceed 260 fsw.

9.3 Equipment and Gas Quality Requirements

9.3.1 Equipment Standards.
    A. Equipment requirements shall be developed and approved by the NDCSB, and met by divers, prior to engaging in mixed-gas diving.

B. Equipment shall meet other pertinent requirements set forth elsewhere in this Manual.

9.3.2 Gas Standards.
A. The quality of inert gases used to produce breathing mixtures shall be of an acceptable grade for human consumption.
B. All mixed gases must be analyzed by the diver using the mixture.
C. Gas analysis must be accomplished by analyzing the fractions of each individual gas component in the mixture, less one. Thus, if Heliox is used, this requirement is met by measuring the FO_2. If Trimix (O_2, N_2, He) is used, at least two (2) components must be analyzed, typically oxygen and helium.

9.4 Operational Requirements

9.4.1 General.
A. Diving projects involving the use of equipment other than open circuit design, use of gas mixtures other than air or Nitrox, or outside the no-decompression limits must be approved by the NDCSB before diving activities begin.
B. If a period of more than 6 months has elapsed since the last mixed gas dive, a series of progressive workup dives to return the diver(s) to proficiency status prior to the start of project diving operations is recommended.

9.4.2 Oxygen Parameters and Considerations.
A. The maximum PO_2 to be used for planning required decompression dives is 1.6 ATA. It is recommended that a PO_2 of less than 1.6 ATA be used during bottom exposure.
B. Maximum planned Oxygen Tolerance Units (OTU) will be considered based on mission duration.
C. Divers decompressing on high-oxygen concentration mixtures shall closely monitor one another for signs of CNS oxygen toxicity.
D. Only NDCSB approved algorithms and computers may be used for mixed gas diving.

Section 10:   REBREATHERS

10.1   General

10.1.1 Scope and Application.
  A. This section defines specific requirements for the use of rebreathers, training and/or experience verification, equipment, and operational and additional safety protocols to be used.
  B. Application of this standard is in addition to pertinent requirements of all other sections contained within this Manual.
  C. For rebreather dives that also involve staged decompression and/or mixed gas diving, all requirements for each of the relevant diving modes shall be met.
  D. Instructors shall be qualified for the type of training to be provided. Training shall be conducted by agencies or instructors approved by the NDCSB.

10.1.2 Approval Process.
  A. No diver shall conduct planned operations using rebreathers without prior review and approval of the NDCSB.
  B. The NDCSB will review each application for specialized rebreather diving, and may include any further requirements deemed necessary beyond those listed here on a case-by-case basis.

10.2   Minimum Experience and Training Requirements

10.2.1 Prerequisites.
  A. General.
    1) Specific training requirements for the use of each rebreather model shall be approved by the NDCSB on a case-by-case basis.
    2) Training shall include factory-recommended requirements, but may exceed these to prepare for the type of mission intended (e.g., staged decompression or Heliox/Trimix Closed-Circuit Rebreather diving).
  B. Requirements.
    1) Active scientific diver status, with depth qualification sufficient for the planned application.
    2) Completion of a minimum of 50 open water dives on open circuit SCUBA.
    3) A minimum 130 fsw depth qualification to ensure the diver is sufficiently conversant with the complications of deeper diving. If the sole expected application for the use of rebreathers is shallower than this, a lesser depth qualification may be allowed with the approval of the NDCSB.
    4) Nitrox training. Training in the use of Nitrox mixtures containing 25 percent to 40 percent oxygen is required. Training in the use of mixtures containing 40 percent to 100 percent oxygen may be required, as needed for the planned application and rebreather system. Nitrox training may be provided as part of rebreather training.

10.2.2 Academic Training.
  A. Successful completion of the following training program qualifies the diver for rebreather diving using the system on which the diver was trained, in depths of 130 fsw and shallower, for dives that do not require decompression, and using nitrogen/oxygen breathing media.

B. Satisfactory completion of a rebreather training program authorized or recommended by the manufacturer of the rebreather to be used, or other training approved by the NDCSB. Successful completion of training does not in itself authorize the diver to use rebreathers. The diver must demonstrate to the NDCSB that he/she possesses the proper attitude, judgment, and discipline to safely conduct rebreather diving in the context of planned operations.

C. Classroom training shall include:

1) A review of diving physics and physiology, decompression management, and dive planning included in prior scientific diver, Nitrox, staged decompression and/or mixed gas training, as they pertain to the safe operation of the selected rebreather system and planned diving application.

2) In particular, causes, signs and symptoms, first aid, treatment and prevention of the following must be covered:
    a) Hyperoxia (CNS and Pulmonary Oxygen Toxicity);
    b) Middle Ear Oxygen Absorption Syndrome (oxygen ear);
    c) Hyperoxic myopia;
    d) Hypoxia;
    e) Hypercapnia;
    f) Inert gas narcosis;
    g) Decompression sickness;
    h) Caustic cocktail;
    i) Allergic reactions; and
    j) Disease transmission.

3) Rebreather-specific information required for the safe and effective operation of the system to be used, including system design and operation, for the following:
    a) Counterlung(s);
    b) CO_2 scrubber;
    c) CO_2 absorbent material types, activity characteristics, storage, handling and disposal;
    d) Oxygen control system types and designs;
    e) Diluent control system types and designs (if any).

4) Pre-dive set-up and testing

5) Post-dive break-down and maintenance

6) Oxygen exposure management

7) Decompression management and applicable decompression tracking methods

8) Dive operations planning

9) Problem recognition and management, including system failures leading to hypoxia, hyperoxia, hypercapnia, flooded loop, and caustic cocktail

10) Emergency protocols and bailout procedures

10.2.3 Practical Training.
    A. A minimum number of hours of underwater time.

Type	Pool/Confined Water	O/W Training	O/W Supervised
Oxygen Rebreather	1 dive, 90 min[1]	4 dives, 120 min[1]	2 dives, 60 min[1]
Semi-Closed Circuit	1 dive, 90-120 min	4 dives, 120 min[2]	4 dives, 120 min[2]
Closed-Circuit	1 dive, 90-120 min	8 dives, 380 min[3]	4 dives, 240 min[3]

Notes:
[1] Dives should not exceed 20 fsw.
[2] First two dives should not exceed 60 fsw. Subsequent dives should be to progressively greater depths, with at least one (1) dive between 100 - 130 fsw.
[3] Total underwater time (pool and open water) of approximately 500 minutes. First two (2) open water dives should not exceed 60 fsw. Subsequent dives should be to progressively greater depths, with at least two (2) dives between 100 - 130 fsw.

    B. Amount of required in-water time should increase proportionally with the complexity of rebreather system used.
    C. Training shall be in accordance with the manufacturer's recommendations.

10.2.4 Practical Evaluations.
    A. Upon completion of practical training, the diver must demonstrate to the NDCSB proficiency in pre-dive, dive, and post-dive operational procedures for the particular model of rebreather to be used.
    B. Skills shall include, at a minimum:
        1) Oxygen control system calibration and operation checks;
        2) Carbon dioxide absorbent canister packing;
        3) Supply gas cylinder analysis and pressure check;
        4) Test of one-way valves;
        5) System assembly and breathing loop leak testing;
        6) Pre-dive breathing to test system operation;
        7) In-water leak checks;
        8) Buoyancy control during descent, bottom operations, and ascent;
        9) System monitoring and control during descent, bottom operations, and ascent;
       10) Proper interpretation and operation of system instrumentation (e.g., PO_2 displays, dive computers, gas supply pressure gauges, alarms) as applicable);
       11) Unit donning and doffing on the surface;
       12) Bailout and emergency procedures for self and buddy, including:
           a) System malfunction recognition and solution
           b) Manual system control
           c) Flooded breathing loop recovery (if possible)
           d) Absorbent canister failure
           e) Alternate bailout options
       13) Symptom recognition and emergency procedures for hyperoxia, hypoxia, and hypercapnia; and
       14) Proper system maintenance, including:
           a) Full breathing loop disassembly and cleaning (e.g., mouthpiece, check-valves, hoses, counterlung, absorbent canister);
           b) Oxygen sensor replacement (for Semi-Closed Circuit Rebreather and CCR); and
           c) Other tasks required for specific rebreather models.

10.2.5 Written Evaluation. A written evaluation approved by the NDCSB with a pre-determined passing score, covering concepts of both classroom and practical training, is required.

10.2.6 Supervised Rebreather Dives.
    A. Upon successful completion of open water training dives, the diver is authorized to conduct a series of supervised rebreather dives, during which the diver gains additional experience and proficiency.
    B. The supervisor. The supervisor for these dives shall be approved by the NDCSB and should be an active scientific diver experienced in diving with the make/model of rebreather being used.
    C. Dives at this level may be targeted to activities associated with the planned scientific diving application. See the above table for number and cumulative underwater time for different rebreather types.
    D. Maximum ratio of divers per designated dive supervisor is 4:1. The supervisor may dive as part of the planned operations.

10.2.7 Extended Range Diving.
    A. Rebreather dives involving operational depths in excess of 130 fsw, requiring staged decompression, or using diluents containing inert gases other than nitrogen are subject to additional training requirements, as determined by NDCSB on a case-by-case basis. Prior experience with required decompression and mixed gas diving using open circuit SCUBA is desirable, but is not sufficient for transfer to dives using rebreathers without additional training.
    B. As a prerequisite for training in staged decompression on rebreathers using air diluent and not exceeding 130 fsw, the diver shall have logged a minimum of 25 hours of underwater time on the rebreather system to be used, with at least ten (10) rebreather dives in the 100 fsw to 130 fsw range.
    C. As a prerequisite for training for use of rebreathers with gas mixtures containing inert gas other than nitrogen, the diver shall have logged a minimum of 50 hours of underwater time on the rebreather system to be used and shall have completed training in decompression methods using rebreathers. The diver shall have completed at least twelve (12) dives requiring staged decompression on the rebreather model to be used, with at least four (4) dives between130 fsw and 160 fsw.
    D. Training shall be in accordance with standards for decompression and mixed gas diving, as applicable to rebreather systems, starting at the130 fsw level.

10.2.8 Maintenance of Proficiency.
    A. To maintain authorization to dive with rebreathers, an authorized diver shall make at least one (1) dive using a rebreather every 8 weeks. For divers authorized for the conduct of extended range, decompression or mixed-gas diving, at least one (1) dive should be made to a depth near 130 fsw, practicing decompression protocols.
    B. For a diver in arrears, the NDCSB shall approve a program of remedial knowledge and skill tune-up training and a course of dives required to return the diver to full authorization.

10.3   Equipment Requirements

10.3.1 General Requirements.
    A. Only those models of rebreathers specifically approved by NDCSB shall be used.

B. Rebreathers shall be manufactured according to acceptable Quality Control/Quality Assurance protocols, as evidenced by compliance with the essential elements of ISO 9000-9004. Manufacturers should be able to provide to the NDCSB supporting documentation to this effect.

C. Unit performance specifications shall be within acceptable levels as defined by the NDCSB.

D. Prior to approval, the manufacturer shall supply the NDCSB with supporting documentation detailing the methods of specification determination by a recognized third-party testing agency, including unmanned and manned testing. Test data should be from a recognized, independent test facility.

E. A complete instruction manual is required, fully describing the operation of all rebreather components and subsystems as well as maintenance procedures.

F. A maintenance log is required. The unit and subsystem component (i.e., regulators, computers, and cylinders) maintenance shall be up-to-date based upon manufacturer's recommendations.

10.3.2 Minimum Equipment.
A. General.
1) Surface/dive valve in the mouthpiece assembly, allowing sealing of the breathing loop from the external environment when not in use.
2) An automatic diluent addition valve (ADV) or equivalent, so that manual volumetric compensation during descent is unnecessary.
3) Manual gas addition valves, so that manual volumetric compensation during descent and manual oxygen addition are possible at all times during the dive.
4) The diver shall carry an alternate life support capability (e.g., open circuit bailout) sufficient to allow the solution of minor problems, allow reliable access to a pre-planned alternate life support system or allow ascent to the surface.

B. Oxygen Rebreathers. Oxygen rebreathers shall be equipped with manual and automatic gas addition valves.

C. Semi-Closed Circuit Rebreathers.
1) SCRs shall be equipped with at least one manufacturer-approved oxygen sensor sufficient to warn the diver of impending hypoxia.
2) Sensor redundancy is desirable, but not required.

D. Closed Circuit Rebreathers.
1) CCRs shall have three oxygen sensors.
2) A minimum of two independent displays of oxygen sensor readings shall be available to the diver.
3) Two independent power supplies in the rebreather design are desirable. If only one is present, a secondary system to monitor oxygen levels without power from the primary battery must be incorporated.
4) CCR shall be equipped with manual diluent and oxygen addition valves to enable the diver to maintain safe oxygen levels in the event of failure of the primary power supply or automatic gas addition systems.

E. Redundancies in onboard electronics, power supplies, and life support systems are highly desirable.

10.4   Operational Requirements

10.4.1 General Requirements.

A. All dives involving rebreathers must comply with applicable operational requirements for open circuit SCUBA dives to equivalent depths and decompression schedules.

B. No rebreather system shall be used in situations beyond the manufacturer's stated design limits (e.g., dive depth, duration, and water temperature).

C. Modifications to rebreather systems shall be in compliance with manufacturer's recommendations.

D. Rebreather maintenance is to be in compliance with manufacturer's recommendations including sanitizing, replacement of consumables (e.g., sensors, CO_2 absorbent, gas, batteries) and periodic maintenance.

E. Dive Plan. In addition to specialized dive plan components stipulated in Section 4.1.2 of this Manual, all dive plans that include the use of rebreathers must include, at a minimum, the following details:

    1) Information about the specific rebreather including make, model, and type of rebreather system to be used, and other specific details as requested by the NDCSB;

    2) Type of CO_2 absorbent material;

    3) Composition and volume(s) of supply gases; and

    4) Description of alternate bailout procedures to be employed, including manual rebreather operation and open circuit procedures.

F. No modifications may be made to the life support components of a rebreather without the manufacturer's approval.

10.4.2 Buddy Qualifications.

A. A diver whose buddy is diving with a rebreather shall be trained in basic rebreather operation, hazard identification, and assist/rescue procedures for a rebreather diver.

B. If the buddy of a rebreather diver is using open circuit SCUBA, the rebreather diver must be equipped with a means to provide the open circuit SCUBA diver with a sufficient supply of open circuit breathing gas to allow both divers to return safely to the surface.

10.4.3 Oxygen Exposures.

A. Planned oxygen partial pressure in the breathing gas shall not exceed 1.4 ATA at depths greater than 30 fsw for mixed gas CCRs or 1.6 ATA for oxygen CCR, and mass flow controlled SCR.

B. Planned oxygen partial pressure set point for CCR shall not exceed 1.4 ATA. Set point at depth should be reduced to manage oxygen toxicity according to the NOAA Oxygen Exposure Limits.

C. Oxygen exposures should not exceed the NOAA oxygen single exposure limits or the REPEX limits for the dive operations. Both CNS and pulmonary (whole-body) oxygen exposure indices should be tracked for each diver.

10.4.4 Decompression Management.

A. The NDCSB shall review and approve the method of decompression management selected for a given diving application and project.

B. Decompression management can be safely achieved by a variety of methods, depending on the type and model of rebreather to be used. The following is a general list of methods for different rebreather types:

    1) Oxygen rebreathers: Not applicable.

    2) Constant mass flow SCR (presumed constant FO_2):

        a) Use of any method approved for open circuit SCUBA diving breathing air, above the maximum operational depth of the supply gas.

      b) Use of open circuit Nitrox dive tables based upon exertion level of 2.5 liters per minute oxygen consumption. In this case, contingency air dive tables may be necessary for active-addition SCRs in the event that exertion level is higher than expected.

      c) Equivalent air depth correction to open circuit air dive tables, based upon exertion level of 2.5 LPM oxygen consumption for planned exertion level, gas supply rate, and gas composition. In this case, contingency air dive tables may be necessary for active-addition SCRs in the event that exertion level is higher than expected.

   3) CCR (constant PO_2):

      a) Integrated constant PO_2 dive computer.

      b) Non-integrated constant PO_2 dive computer.

      c) Constant PO_2 dive tables.

      d) Open circuit (constant FO_2) dive computer set to inspired FO_2 predicted using PO_2 set point at the maximum planned dive depth.

      e) EAD correction to standard open circuit air dive tables, based on the inspired FO_2 predicted using the PO_2 set point at the maximum planned dive depth.

      f) Air dive computer, or air dive tables used above for the MOD of air for the selected PO_2 setpoint.

10.4.5 Logs and Checklists.

A. Logs and checklists will be developed for the rebreather used, and will be used before and after every dive. The diver and a witness shall indicate by initial on the checklist that an inspection was performed prior to dive. Divers shall indicate by initialing that checklists have been completed before and after each dive. Such documents shall be filed and maintained as permanent project records.

B. No rebreather shall be dived which has failed any portion of the pre-dive check, or is found to not be operating in accordance with manufacturer's specifications.

C. Pre-dive checks shall include:

   1) Gas supply cylinders filled to adequate pressure for the anticipated dive, leaving a reserve gas supply of at least 500 psi in each individual gas cylinder upon surfacing;

   2) Composition of all supply and bailout gases analyzed and documented;

   3) Oxygen sensors calibrated;

   4) Carbon dioxide canister properly packed;

   5) Remaining duration of canister life recorded;

   6) Breathing loop assembled;

   7) Positive and negative pressure leak checks;

   8) Automatic volume addition system working;

   9) Automatic oxygen addition systems working;

   10) With unit turned on (i.e., electronics controlling the unit), pre-breathe system for an adequate duration to confirm operation of sensor readings and automatic oxygen addition, (at least 5 minutes in water colder than 40°F to ensure proper oxygen addition and carbon dioxide removal (be alert for signs of hypoxia or hypercapnia;

   11) Other procedures specific to the model of rebreather used;

   12) Documentation of ALL components assembled; and

   13) Final operational verification immediately before entering the water including:

      a) PO_2 in the rebreather is not hypoxic;

      b) Oxygen addition system is functioning;

      c) Volumetric addition is functioning;

d) Bailout life support is functioning;
e) BCD is functioning;
f) Displays are functioning;
g) Electronics are on;
h) All gas cylinder valves are open; and
i) Bubble check upon entering the water.

10.4.6 Alternate Life Support System.
A. The diver shall have reliable access to an alternate life support system designed to safely return the diver to the surface at normal ascent rates, including any required decompression in the event of primary rebreather failure.
B. The complexity and extent of such systems are directly related to the depth/time profiles of the mission. Examples of such systems include, but are not limited to:
1) Open circuit bailout cylinders or sets of cylinders, either carried or pre-positioned;
2) Redundant rebreather; and
3) Pre-positioned life support equipment with topside support.

10.4.7 CO_2 Absorbent Material.
A. CO_2 absorption canister shall be filled in accordance with the manufacturer's specifications.
B. CO_2 absorbent material shall be used in accordance with the manufacturer's specifications for expected duration.
C. Unspent CO_2 absorbent material remaining in the canister following a dive must be discarded after 12 hours from initial filling, or according to the manufacturer's specification, whichever comes first.
D. Long-term storage of carbon dioxide absorbents shall be in a cool, dry location in a sealed container. Field storage must be adequate to maintain viability of material until use.

10.4.8 Consumables. Other consumables (e.g., batteries, oxygen sensors) shall be maintained, tested, and replaced in accordance with the manufacturer's specifications.

10.4.9 Disinfecting Units.
A. The entire breathing loop, including mouthpiece, hoses, counterlungs, and CO_2 canister, shall be disinfected periodically according to manufacturer's specifications.
B. The loop must be disinfected between each use of the same rebreather by different divers.

10.5 Oxygen Rebreathers

10.5.1 Depth Limits. Oxygen rebreathers shall not be used at depths greater than 20 fsw.

10.5.2 Flushing of Breathing Loop.
A. Breathing loop and diver's lungs must be adequately flushed with pure oxygen prior to entering the water on each dive. Once done, the diver must breathe continuously and solely from the intact loop, or re-flushing is required.
B. Breathing loop shall be flushed with fresh oxygen prior to ascending to avoid hypoxia due to inert gas in the loop.

C. If a repetitive dive is conducted on an oxygen rebreather following an open circuit air dive, the loop shall be flushed every 15 minutes during the dive for the first hour, to eliminate any dissolved inert gas diffusing from the body.

10.6   Semi-Closed Circuit Rebreathers

10.6.1 Oxygen Parameters and Considerations.
A. The composition of the injection gas supply of a semi-closed circuit rebreather shall be chosen such that the partial pressure of oxygen in the breathing loop will not drop below 0.2 ATA, even at maximum exertion at the surface.
B. The gas addition rate of active addition SCRs (e.g., Draeger Dolphin and similar units) shall be checked before every dive to ensure it is balanced against expected workload and supply gas FO_2.
C. The intermediate pressure of supply gas delivery system in active-addition SCRs shall be checked periodically for compliance with manufacturer's recommendations.
D. Maximum operating depth shall be based upon the FO_2 in the active supply cylinder.

10.6.2 Flushing of Breathing Loop.
A. Prior to ascent to the surface, the diver shall flush the breathing loop with fresh gas or switch to an open circuit system to avoid hypoxia.
B. The flush should be at a depth of approximately 30 fsw during ascent on dives deeper than 30 fsw, and at bottom depth on dives 30 fsw and shallower.

10.7   Mixed Gas Closed-Circuit Rebreathers

10.7.1 Oxygen Parameters and Considerations.
A. The FO_2 of each diluent gas supply used shall be chosen so that, if breathed directly while in the depth range for which its use is intended, it will produce an inspired PO_2 greater than 0.20 ATA but no greater than 1.1 ATA unless approved by the DM/LD in very limited circumstances during mixed gas diving operations.
B. MOD shall be based on the FO_2 of the diluent in use during each phase of the dive, so as not to exceed a PO_2 limit of 1.1 ATA.
C. The PO_2 set point shall not be lower than 0.4 ATM or higher than 1.4 ATA.

10.7.2 Monitoring of Oxygen Parameters. Divers shall monitor both primary and secondary oxygen display systems at regular intervals throughout the dive, to verify readings are within limits, redundant displays are providing similar values, and whether readings are dynamic or static (as an indicator of sensor failure).

SECTION 11: EMERGENCY PROCEDURES

11.1 Dive Accident Management

11.1.1 General.
  A. Dive accident management includes accident prevention and the development of a DEAP that includes procedures for the emergency care of victims after an accident.
  B. Diving accident management involves activating a DEAP that includes, but is not be limited to:
    1) Stabilization of life sustaining functions;
    2) Administering oxygen; and
    3) Contacting medical personnel and suggested services for assistance and advice.

11.1.2 Diving Emergency Procedures.
  A. The DM or LD shall have the ultimate on-site authority for management of diving related accidents and injuries, unless a DMO or DMT is available.
  B. Each DM or LD will develop a DEAP.
    1) A standardized form (NOAA Diving Emergency Assistance Plan) template has been developed for this purpose (Appendix 4). An electronic version can be downloaded from the NDC website at: www.ndc.noaa.gov.
    2) The DEAP shall be submitted to the UDS as follows:
      a) Annually, as specified by the UDS; or
      b) If the DEAP changes for any reason (e.g., diving is conducted in a different geographic region).
    3) An approved copy of the DEAP shall be made available to all divers and support personnel at the dive location for the duration of the operation.
    4) The UDS shall submit a copy of each unique DEAP to ndp.diveplans@noaa.gov.

11.1.3 Medical Consultation.
  A. Medical advice shall be sought from a qualified health care provider at the first sign or report of a hyperbaric related injury or illness.
  B. Medical advice from a qualified health care provider shall only be changed or modified when:
    1) Contradicting instructions are received from a consulting DMO or hyperbaric physician; or
    2) Life threatening situations requiring immediate on-site deviation. A written record of the deviation shall be made and the NDP DMO briefed as soon as possible after the change.
  C. Initial consult for NOAA related diving maladies shall be attempted with the NDP DMO.
  D. Secondary consult for NOAA related diving maladies when the NDP DMO is not available.
    1) NOAA ships with a DM onboard may consult with the on-call DMO at the Navy Diving and Salvage Training Center (NDSTC) or Navy Experimental Dive Unit (NEDU), Panama City, FL.
    2) NOAA ships without a DMO onboard shall consult with the on-call DMO at the NDCSTC or NEDU.
    3) All other units shall contact DAN, Durham, NC.
  E. Contact information for both the primary and secondary consults shall be listed on the DEAP and verified prior to commencing diving operations.

F. The NOAA Dive Accident Management Field Reference Guide should be used to document information needed to relay to the NDP DMO prior to establishing communications with medical personnel. An electronic version can be downloaded from the NDC website at: www.ndc.noaa.gov.

11.2   Emergency Protocols

11.2.1 General Procedures for Treatment of Hyperbaric Maladies.
A. Details on how to diagnose and report hyperbaric maladies can be found in the NOAA Dive Accident Management Field Reference Guide.
B. Treatment for hyperbaric maladies will be performed in accordance with current medical standards as prescribed by the NDP DMO.
C. Qualified personnel within the scope of their training and certification level/status are authorized to perform the protocols listed in this section as indicated for signs or symptoms of decompression illness.

11.2.2 Medical Instructions for Conscious Patients. The following procedures may be used for the treatment of a conscious diver when a DMO is not available at the dive location and the provider is trained in these procedures:
A. Check ABC's;
B. Administer 100 percent oxygen;
C. Remove exposure suit, dry patient, and keep warm;
D. Place patient in position of comfort;
E. Take vital signs every 5 minutes if unstable and every 15 minutes if stable;
F. Gather dive history info from diver, buddy and/or eyewitnesses;
G. Perform field neurological exam;
H. Contact NDP DMO and Emergency Medical Services (EMS) as soon as possible;
I. Administer 0.5 liters of water orally per hour for 2 hours, and then reduce to 100-200 milliliters (ml) per hour thereafter;
J. If unable to drink sufficient quantities of fluids orally, start IV with Lactated Ringers or Normal Saline (0.9 percent NaCl), and administer 0.5 liters per hour for 2 hours, then reduce to 100-200 ml per hour thereafter; and
K. If unable to urinate 30 cc/hour voluntarily, insert Foley catheter and monitor urine output quantity and appearance.

11.2.3 Medical Instructions for Unconscious Patients. The following procedures may be used for the treatment of an unconscious diver when a DMO is not available at the dive location and the provider is trained in these procedures:
A. Check ABC's;
B. Administer 100 percent oxygen;
C. Remove exposure suit, dry patient, and keep warm;
D. Place patient on their left side with the right thigh and knee drawn up;
E. Take vital signs every 5 minutes if unstable and every 15 minutes if stable;
F. Gather dive history info from dive buddy and/or eyewitnesses;
G. Perform field neurological exam and Glascow Coma Scale evaluation;
H. Contact NDP DMO and EMS as soon as possible;
I. Start IV with Lactated Ringers or Normal Saline; administer 0.5 L per hour for 2 hours; then reduce to 100-200 ml per hour thereafter; and
J. Insert Foley catheter and monitor urine output quantity and appearance.

11.2.4 No Hyperbaric Chamber at Dive Location. If there is no hyperbaric chamber available at the dive location, initiate the following protocol:
  A. Conduct field neurological exam and gather data for medical consultation;
  B. Administer 100 percent oxygen;
  C. Contact medical personnel for assistance and advice as soon as possible as outlined in Section 11.1.3;
  D. Administer medications, drugs, and fluids as directed by the NDP DMO, or designee;
  E. Follow other specific directions, recommendations, and precautions concerning the treatment and/or evacuation as medically directed or within the scope of training and certification level/status;
  F. If there is a change in signs or symptoms after 30 minutes of oxygen breathing, continue 100 percent oxygen, consult a diving physician, and begin evacuation to a hyperbaric chamber; and
  G. If there is no change in signs or symptoms after 30 minutes, the diver may be taken off oxygen and observed for 1 hour. Re-examine diver every 2-6 hours thereafter.

11.2.5 Hyperbaric Chamber at Dive Location. The following procedures may be used for the treatment of decompression illness in the event a qualified DMO is not available at the chamber:
  A. Type I Decompression Sickness (DCS).
    1) Place diver on 100 percent oxygen and contact the NDP DMO, or designee for instructions prior to pressurizing the diver in a hyperbaric chamber.
    2) If neither the NDP DMO nor his/her designee can be contacted immediately, or signs or symptoms indicate progression to Type II DCS, pressurize diver to 60 fsw (2.8 ATA) and begin a USN TT6. If still unable to contact the NDP DMO, or designee, continue USN TT6 until completion and then inform the DMO as soon as possible.
  B. Type II DCS or AGE.
    1) Place diver on 100 percent oxygen and immediately pressurize diver to 60 fsw (2.8 ATA) and begin a USN TT6. Contact the NDP DMO, or designee, as soon as possible for further instructions.
    2) If neither the NDP DMO nor his/her designee can be contacted immediately, or signs or symptoms indicate progression to Type II DCS, pressurize diver to 60 fsw (2.8 ATA) and begin a USN TT6.
  C. Standing medical orders for divers undergoing hyperbaric treatment.
    1) If the diver is able to take oral fluids but is not voiding at least 60-90 cc per hour (2-3 ounces), increase fluid intake.
    2) If the diver is unable to take oral fluids, start IV with Lactated Ringers or Normal Saline and administer 500 cc immediately, and then infuse at 100-125 cc per hour.
    3) If diver is uncooperative or unable to void, start a Foley catheter with urine output goal of 60-90 cc/hour (2-3 ounces), increase fluid intake if necessary.
    4) Repeat field neurological exam every 15 minutes during the treatment.
    5) If victim is unconscious and does not regain consciousness once at depth, start an NG tube.

11.2.6 Guidelines for Non-Standard Scenarios. The following guidelines are provided to aid the chamber supervisor/operator and DMO in responding to non-standard problems that are not addressed elsewhere.
  A. Inability to equalize ears during pressurization of the chamber. Conscious victim determined to have:

          1) Type I DCS.
            a) Stop descent, ascend a few feet and try equalizing.
            b) If still unable to clear after several tries, return chamber to surface and administer a nasal decongestant spray.
            c) Wait until patient is able to auto-inflate their middle ear, then repeat attempt of pressurization in chamber.
          2) Type II DCS or Arterial Gas Embolism (AGE).
            a) Conscious victim: Depending on the symptoms the chamber supervisor may elect to try one or more of the steps listed above.
            b) Unconscious victim: Do not delay; begin pressurization to 60 fsw in the chamber immediately.
      B. Confined Space Anxiety Syndrome (Claustrophobia).
          1) Try to calm and reassure patient; and
          2) If necessary, the DMO may direct the administration of an anti-anxiety agent to the patient orally.

11.2.7 Post-Treatment Procedures.
      A. Repeat neurological exams should be conducted at the conclusion of treatment followed by exams 1 and 6 hours following treatment and intervals of 6 hours thereafter, or as advised by the consulting DMO, until diver is seen by a physician.
      B. Patients treated for Type I decompression sickness symptoms with complete resolution will be advised to report to a medical facility for medical examination upon completion of the recompression treatment.
      C. Immediate transportation of the patient to a medical facility for medical examination following hyperbaric treatment is required when:
          1) Directed by the consulting DMO;
          2) Treatment was for Type II or AGE symptoms, or;
          3) Residual symptoms continue after treatment.

11.2.8 Temporary Suspension from Diving.
      A. Divers treated for any pulmonary barotrauma or decompression related illness shall not engage in diving activities involving hyperbaric exposures until approved (in writing) by the NDP DMO.
      B. For further guidance on returning to diving after decompression sickness, refer to the NDMSPM.

11.2.9 Other Emergency Considerations. In addition to diving concerns, DMs and LDs should also consider emergency procedures for fire fighting, adverse environmental conditions, illness, and injury and include these in their dive planning and pre-dive briefing.

SECTION 12: RECORDKEEPING AND REPORTING REQUIREMENTS

12.1 Recordkeeping

12.1.1 General. The NDC shall maintain permanent records for each certified NOAA Diver including, but not limited to:
A. Evidence of certification level;
B. Training;
C. Log sheets;
D. Results of current physical examination;
E. Reports of disciplinary actions by the NDCSB;
F. First aid, CPR, including adult AED, and oxygen delivery certifications; and
G. Other pertinent information deemed necessary by the NDCSB.

12.1.2 Unit Training Log. Each unit shall maintain a current record of training conducted at the unit level for ease of tracking and verification by DUSA inspectors.

12.1.3 Availability of Records.
A. Upon the request of the Assistant Secretary of Labor [for OSHA], or the Director, National Institute for Occupational Safety and Health, Department of Health and Human Services, or their designees; the employer shall make available for inspection and copying any record or document required by this standard.
B. Records and documents required by 29 CFR 1910, Subpart T shall be provided upon request to employees, designated representatives, and the Assistant Secretary in accordance with 29 CFR 1910.1020 (a)-(e) and (g)-(i) (in 1996, 29 CFR 1910.20 was re-designated as 29 CFR 1910.1020).
C. Safe practices manuals (29 CFR 1910.420), depth-time profiles (29 CFR 1910.422), decompression procedure assessment evaluations (29 CFR 1910.423), and records of hospitalizations (29 CFR 1910.440) shall be provided in the same manner as employee exposure records or analyses using exposure or medical records.
D. Equipment inspections and testing records which pertain to employees (29 CFR 1910.430) shall also be provided upon request to employees and their designated representatives.
E. Except as prohibited by the Health Insurance Portability and Accountability Act of 1996 (HIPAA) privacy rule or other law, copies of NDC records are available for review by the NDSO, SECO, NDC personnel and the NDP chain of command.
F. Medical records belonging to an individual diver or former diver shall be made available to that individual upon written request.
G. Medical records may also be provided to the attending physician of a diver or former diver when released in writing by the diver.

12.1.4 Retention of Records.

A. The following records shall be retained for the following minimum periods:

Record	Period at NDC	Period at Diving Units
Pre- and Post-Dive Checklists	3 years if included in a Diving Incident Report Case File then forwarded to Federal Record Center and kept for 72 years then destroyed	24 hours post operation except following a reportable diving injury and then include in Diving Incident Report Case File
Dive Plan	1 year except following a reportable diving injury then included in Diving Incident Report Case File	24 hours post operation then forward to ndp.diveplans@noaa.gov
Diving Emergency Assistance Plans	1 year except following a reportable diving injury then included in Diving Incident Report Case File	Filed at ndp.diveplans@noaa.gov on an annual basis or when the information on the DEAP changes (e.g., geographically or seasonally).
Diver medical records	3 years then forwarded to Federal Record Center and kept for 72 years then destroyed	
NOAA Diving Standards and Safety Manuals	Current and all previous manuals	Current manual only
On-site Supervisor's Dive Log	Permanently	24 hours post operation
On-line Dive Log	Permanently	
Dive Incident Report	Permanently	
Equipment inspection and testing	Current entry or until removed from service except following a reportable diving injury then included in Diving Incident Report Case File	Current entry or until removed from service except following a reportable diving injury then included in Diving Incident Report Case File
Records of hospitalizations	Permanently	
SEP Off-Duty Proficiency Dive Skill Checklist	3 years if included in a Diving Incident Report Case File then forwarded to Federal Record Center and kept for 72 years then destroyed	30 days post dive except following a reportable diving injury and then include in Diving Incident Report Case File
NOAA Diver Agreement for Use of NOAA Issued Diving Equipment Off-Duty	3 years if included in a Diving Incident Report Case File then forwarded to Federal Record Center and kept for 72 years then destroyed	30 days post dive except following a reportable diving injury and then include in Diving Incident Report Case File
Assumption of Risk and Release of Liability for Use of SEP gear Off-Duty	3 years if included in a Diving Incident Report Case File then forwarded to Federal Record Center and kept for 72 years then destroyed	30 days post dive except following a reportable diving injury and then include in Diving Incident Report Case File

B. After the expiration of the retention period of any record, the record may be further retained or destroyed at the discretion of the NDPM and in accordance with 29 CFR 1910.1020 (h) and the appropriate NOAA Records Disposition Schedule.

C. In the event the NOAA ceases to do business:
1) The successor employer shall receive and retain all dive and employee medical records required by this standard, or;
2) If there is no successor employer, dive and employee medical records shall be forwarded to the National Institute for Occupational Safety and Health, Department of Health and Human Services.

12.1.5 Logging of Dives.
A. The NDP Supervisor's Dive Log (or analogous form) must be used to log all duty dives and must be kept on site for no less than 24 hours post operation.
B. All NOAA divers are required to log all official dives and are encouraged to log all non-duty dives.
C. Dives are to be logged as soon as possible after completion using the web-based recording system available on the NDC website.
D. Non-duty dives performed to fulfill diving proficiency requirements shall also be logged.
E. A dive is defined as the time spent breathing compressed gas underwater or in a hyperbaric chamber and is considered completed when an individual returns to surface pressure and remains for a minimum of 10 minutes.
F. The following information shall be recorded and maintained for each diving operation:
1) Names of dive team members including DM or LD;
2) Date, time, and location;
3) Diving modes used;
4) Breathing gases used;
5) Type of dive (i.e. Working or Scientific);
6) Type of equipment used;
7) Dive platform;
8) Tasks performed;
9) Approximate underwater and surface conditions (visibility, water temperature and current);
10) Maximum depth and bottom time for each diver;
11) Decompression mode (tables or dive computer); and
12) Depth and duration of safety stop (if performed).

12.2 Reporting Diving Incidents

12.2.1 General.
A. All diving related incidents shall be investigated, documented and reported to NOAA management in accordance with NAO 209-1 and NAO 209-123. Both policies are available online, at SECO and NDC websites respectively.
B. Reporting requirements vary with incidents involving injury or non-injury.
C. All diving related incidents and near-misses occurring while performing official NOAA duties shall be reported to SECO via their website, www.seco.noaa.gov with the exception of OMAO vessels which will use MOC-137.

12.2.2 Reportable Diving Injuries.
 A. NOAA shall record the occurrence of any OSHA "recordable" diving related injury or illness requiring medical treatment beyond basic first aid, specifying the circumstances of the incident and the extent of any injuries or illnesses.
 B. NOAA shall record and report occupational injuries and illnesses in accordance with NOAA and OSHA incident reporting procedures.
 C. If pressure related injuries are suspected, or if symptoms are evident, the following additional information shall be recorded and retained with the record of the dive for a period of 5 years by the NDC:
  1) NOAA Dive Incident Report form, and
  2) Written descriptive report to include:
   a) Name, address, phone numbers of principal parties involved;
   b) Summary of experience of divers involved;
   c) Location, description of dive site, and description of conditions that led up to incident;
   d) Description of symptoms, including depth and time of onset;
   e) Description and results of treatment;
   f) Disposition of case; and
   g) Recommendations to avoid reoccurrence of similar incident.
 D. Examples of reportable diving injuries include:
  1) Fatalities;
  2) Injuries requiring hyperbaric therapy (e.g., decompression sickness and lung overexpansion injuries); and
  3) Injuries requiring hospitalization of 24 hours or more, medical care beyond basic first aid, or that impair an individual's ability to dive for more than 48 hours. See Appendix 14.
 E. Reporting Procedures.
  1) Divers shall:
   a) Notify the DM or LD immediately at the first sign or symptom of any injuries sustained during diving operations;
   b) Notify immediate work supervisor; and
   c) Complete the employee section of the Office of Worker's Compensation Programs (OWCP) Form CA-1 (Federal employees only) and forward to immediate work supervisor within 24 hours of being released from medical care. Note: NOAA Corps Officers who suffer an injury are not required to submit an OWCP CA-1 form.
  2) Immediate work supervisors shall:
   a) Report incident via the on-line NOAA Accident/Incident Reporting Form (www.seco.noaa.gov) or the MOC-137 when occurring on an OMAO vessel, within 24 hours of the incident; and
   b) Complete the supervisors section of the Form CA-1 (For NOAA employees, with the exception of NOAA Corps Officers, and where medical costs were incurred) and forward all original documents to Contract Claims Services, Inc. for processing.
  3) DMs and LDs shall:
   a) Immediately notify their respective UDS of the reportable injury; and
   b) Submit a written incident report to their UDS within 7 calendar days of the reportable injury.
  4) UDSs shall:
   a) Immediately notify their respective LODO/SODO of the reportable injury; and

b) Submit a detailed analysis and report of the reportable injury to the respective LODO/SODO within 7 calendar days of receipt of report.

c) The reports shall include, but not be limited to, the following: nature of the operations; existing environmental conditions; dive profiles; dive plans; personnel involved; type of equipment used; nature of any equipment failures; causal analyses that indicates both immediate and basic (root) causes; recommendations for prevention of future injuries; a copy of the DM's or LD's incident narrative; a copy of any relevant medical records from treatment received from the treated diver; a copy of the NDP Dive Incident Report; and a copy of the SECO on-line incident report.

5) LODOs/SODO (or DLODOs/DSODO) shall:

a) Immediately notify the NDPM of the reportable injury;

b) Conduct a fact-finding investigation into the incident and forward final report to the NDPM within 10 calendar days of receipt of report from UDS; and

c) Include a copy and an analysis of the report submitted by the UDS; a conclusion as to the cause of the incident; and a corrective action plan (if deemed appropriate).

6) NDPM shall:

a) Review the report for completeness and any immediate mitigation actions required to prevent a similar event from occurring; and

b) Forward copy of report to the Chair of the NDCSB, the Chair of the NDMRB and NDSO for review within 7 calendar days of receipt of report from LODO/SODO.

7) Chair of the NDMRB shall:

a) Forward copies of the report to the members of the NDMRB within 7 calendar days of receipt of report from NDPM;

b) Consolidate comments received from NDMRB members; and

c) Forward comments to the NDPM and Chair, NDCSB.

8) Chair of the NDCSB shall:

a) Forward copies of the report to the members of the NDCSB within 7 calendar days of receipt of report from NDPM;

b) Consolidate comments received from the NDCSB members;

c) Obtain consensus from the NDCSB of any corrective actions required;

d) Discuss incident and corrective actions and direct the NDPM to develop and track corrective actions determined by the NDCSB.

e) The NDCSB will ensure that appropriate individuals or offices are assigned responsibility for completion of the corrective actions; and

f) NDPM will report status of corrective actions to the NDCSB.

12.2.3 Reportable Diving Incidents Not Involving Injuries.

A. General.

1) Occasionally incidents occur that do not involve reportable injuries, but warrant awareness by NOAA officials. Examples include, but are not limited to:

a) Diving equipment malfunction or failure;

b) "Near miss" or "close call" incidents that could have resulted in a fatality or serious injury to a diver or topside support personnel;

c) Any action that jeopardized a diver's safety or that of a dive buddy; or

d) Evidence of poor judgment by a NOAA diver or supervisor.

2) Any near miss incident shall be treated and investigated as if it were a serious injury.

B. Reporting Requirements.

1) It is the duty and responsibility of anyone experiencing or observing a diving related incident, such as one of those listed above, to immediately report the incident to the DM or LD.
2) The DM or LD will:
   a) Report the incident to the UDS within 24 hours of the occurrence;
   b) If warranted, initiate a safety "stand-down" to review the incident and determine: what happened, why did it happen, what corrective actions are needed to mitigate a similar incident, and if and when dive operations can resume.
3) The UDS will file a "near-miss" incident report using on-line the NOAA Accident/Incident Reporting Form (www.seco.noaa.gov) within 24 hours of receiving the report from the DM or LD.
4) If the incident occurs on an OMAO vessel, the incident will also be reported via MOC-137.

APPENDIX 1

ACRONYMS AND INITIALISMS

ABS	American Bureau of Shipping
acfm	actual cubic feet per minute
AED	Automated External Defibrillators
AGE	Arterial Gas Embolism
ANU	Authorized for Navy Use
ASME	American Society of Mechanical Engineers
ATA	Atmospheres Absolute
BCD	Buoyancy Compensator Devices
BIBS	Built-In-Breathing System
CAO	Chief Administrative Officer
CCR	Closed-Circuit Rebreather
CFR	Code of Federal Regulations
CNS	Central Nervous System
CPR	Cardiopulmonary Resuscitation
DEAP	Diving Emergency Assistance Plan
DAN	Divers Alert Network
DCM	Dive Center Manager
DCS	Decompression Sickness
DM/LD	Divemaster/Lead Diver
DMO	Diving Medical Officer
DO	Diving Officer
DOC	U.S. Department of Commerce
DMT	Diver Medical Technician
DPIC	Designated Person-In-Charge
DSO	Diving Safety Officer
DUI	Diving Unlimited International
DUSA	Diving Unit Safety Assessment
EAD	Equivalent Air Depth
EMS	Emergency Medical Services
END	Equivalent Narcotic Depth
FECA	Federal Employee Compensation Act
fsw	Feet of seawater (or equivalent static pressure head)
FTE	NOAA Full-Time Employee
HIPAA	Health Insurance Portability and Accountability Act
HP	High Pressure
IANTD	International Association of Nitrox and Technical Diving
LODO/SODO	Line/Staff Office Diving Officers
LOR	Letter of Reciprocity
LPM	Liters per minute
MD	Physician
MOD	Maximum Operating Depth
NAO	NOAA Administrative Order
NAUI	National Association of Underwater Instructors
NBDHMT	National Board of Diving and Hyperbaric Medical Technology
NDC	NOAA Dive Center
NDP	NOAA Diving Program
NDPM	NOAA Diving Program Manager

NDCSB	NOAA Diving Control and Safety Board
NDMRB	NOAA Diving Medical Review Board
NDMSPM	NOAA Diving Medical Standards and Procedures Manual
NDSO	NOAA Diving Safety Officer
NDSTC	Navy Diving and Salvage Training Center
NEDU	Navy Experimental Dive Unit
NMFS	National Marine Fisheries Service
NOAA	National Oceanic and Atmospheric Administration
NOS	National Ocean Service
NP	Nurse Practitioner
OAR	Office of Oceanic and Atmospheric Research
OMAO	Office of Marine and Aviation Operations
OPM	Office of Personnel Management
OSHA	Occupational Safety and Health Administration
OUT	Oxygen Tolerance Units
PA	Physician's Assistant
PEPIRB	Personal Emergency Position-Indicating Radio Beacon
PLB	Personal Locator Beacon
psi	Unit of pressure, "pounds per square inch"
psig	Unit of pressure, "pounds per square inch gauge"
PVHO	Pressure Vessel for Human Occupancy
RASS	Reserve Air Supply System
REPEX	Repetitive Excursion
SCR	Semi-closed circuit rebreather
SCUBA	Self-Contained Underwater Breathing Apparatus
SECO	NOAA Safety and Environmental Compliance Office
SEP	Standardized Equipment Program
SMB	Surface Marker Buoy
STE	Special Task Endorsement
TDP	Testing Designated Position
TT	U.S. Navy Treatment Table
UDS	Unit Diving Supervisor
USC	United States Code
USN	U.S. Navy

APPENDIX 2

DEFINITIONS

<u>Air sharing</u>: Joint use of a single air supply between divers who are using independent second stages.

<u>Alternate Air Source Inflator</u>: An additional second stage regulator that is attached to the diver's BCD inflator assembly and is used in the event a dive buddy needs to share air. It also serves as a redundant second stage for the diver.

<u>ATA</u>: "Atmospheres Absolute," total pressure exerted on an object, by a gas or mixture of gases, at a specific depth or elevation, including normal atmospheric pressure.

<u>Bottom Time</u>: The total elapsed time measured in minutes from the time when the diver leaves the surface in descent to the time the diver begins a direct ascent to the surface.

<u>Breath-Hold Diving</u>: A diving mode in which the diver uses no self-contained or surface-supplied air or gas supply.

<u>Buddy Breathing</u>: Two divers sharing a single air source from a single second stage.

<u>Buddy Diver / Buddy System</u>: A second comparably equipped SCUBA diver in the water in constant visual or physical contact and ready to render immediate assistance in an emergency.

<u>Certified Diver</u>: A diver who holds a valid certification from an organizational member or internationally recognized certifying agency.

<u>Controlled Ascent</u>: Any one of several kinds of ascents including normal, swimming, and air sharing ascents where the diver(s) maintain control so a pause or stop can be made during the ascent.

<u>Cylinder</u>: A pressure vessel for the storage of gases.

<u>Decompression Chamber</u>: See hyperbaric chamber.

<u>Decompression Sickness</u>: A condition with a variety of symptoms, which may result from gas bubbles in the tissues of divers after pressure reduction.

<u>Decompression Table</u>: A profile or set of profiles of depth-time relationships for ascent rates and breathing mixtures to be followed after a specific depth-time exposure or exposures.

<u>Designated Person-in-Charge (DPIC)</u>: A person designated by the Divemaster or Lead Diver who is at the dive location, and in charge of all aspects of the dive operation affecting the safety and health of the dive team members.

<u>Dive</u>: A dive is defined as the time spent breathing compressed gas underwater or in a hyperbaric chamber and is considered completed when an individual returns to surface pressure and remains for a minimum of 10 minutes.

<u>Diver</u>: An individual in the water who uses an apparatus which supplies breathing gas at ambient pressure.

Dive Computer: A microprocessor based device which computes a diver's theoretical decompression status in real time by using pressure (depth), breathing gas composition, and time as input to a decompression model, or set of decompression tables, programmed into the device.

Dive Location: A surface or vessel from which a diving operation is conducted.

Divemaster/Lead Diver: An individual designated to direct and oversee diving activities.

Dive Site: Physical location of a diver during a dive.

Dive Team: Divers directly involved in a diving operation including the designated person in charge.

Diving Mode: A type of diving required specific equipment, procedures, and techniques, for example, snorkel, SCUBA, surface-supplied air, or mixed gas.

Diving Safety Officer (DSO): Individual responsible for monitoring the safe conduct of a diving program.

EAD: Equivalent Air Depth (see below).

Enriched Air Nitrox (EANx): A name for a breathing mixture of air and oxygen when the percentage of oxygen exceeds 21 percent. This term is considered synonymous with the term "Nitrox."

Equivalent Air Depth (EAD): The depth at which air will have the same nitrogen partial pressure as the Nitrox or mixed gas mixture being used. This number, expressed in units of feet seawater, will always be less than the actual depth for any enriched air mixture.

Equivalent Narcotic Depth (END): The depth at which the inspired nitrogen partial pressure of a breathing gas mixture other than air equates to that of air at another depth.

FO_2: Fraction of oxygen in a gas mixture by volume, expressed as either a decimal or percentage.

FSW: Feet of seawater, or equivalent static head.

Hyperbaric Chamber: A pressure vessel for human occupancy also called a compression chamber or recompression chamber.

Hyperbaric Conditions: Pressure conditions in excess of normal atmospheric pressure at the dive location.

Lead Diver: Certified scientific diver with experience and training to conduct the diving operation.

Line-Tended Diving: A specialized diving technique whereby divers are connected to the surface via a strength member (line) managed by a trained individual topside.

Mixed Gas: A gas mixture containing proportions greater than 1 percent by volume of an inert gas other than nitrogen.

Mixed-Gas Diving: A diving mode in which the diver is breathing a gas mixture containing proportions greater than 1 percent by volume of an inert gas other than nitrogen.

MOD: Maximum Operating Depth, usually determined as the depth at which the PO_2 for a given gas mixture reaches a predetermined maximum.

Nitrox: Any gas comprised predominately of nitrogen and oxygen, most frequently containing between 21 percent and 40 percent oxygen by volume.

NOAA Appointing Officers: Individuals with authority to approve the hiring of NOAA employees.

NOAA Dive Plan: Written details concerning the dive to be performed including personnel and operational information.

NOAA Divemaster: NOAA divers assigned by the NOAA Line or Staff Office Unit Diving Supervisor to oversee and direct all aspects of a dive operation affecting the safety and health of the dive team members at the dive site.

NOAA Divers: Individuals certified by the NOAA Diving Program Manager to dive and perform work in a hyperbaric environment in support of NOAA's mission. These include NOAA employees (federal full-time and contract employees), reciprocity, and volunteer divers.

NOAA Diving Control and Safety Board: An appointed board of representatives from NOAA's Line and Staff Offices who report jointly to the OMAO Director and NOAA Chief Administrative Officer (CAO) and have autonomous and absolute authority over and promote the safe and effective operations of the NOAA Diving Program.

NOAA Diving Manual: Refers to the NOAA Diving Manual, Diving for Science and Technology, 2001 edition. National Oceanic and Atmospheric Administration, Office of Undersea Research, US Department of Commerce.

NOAA Diving Medical Officer: A health care provider with specialized training in diving and hyperbaric medicine capable of recognizing and providing medical services and/or advice for diving related injuries.

NOAA Diving Program: Group consisting of the Dive Program Manager, NOAA Diving Control and Safety Board, Dive Safety Officer, OMAO Diving Officer, Dive Medical Officer, Line Office Diving Officers and Unit Dive Supervisors who ensure that all NOAA diving operations are conducted safely, efficiently and economically.

NOAA Diving Program Manager: Individual responsible for managing the day-to-day affairs of the NOAA Diving Program and serving as the ranking NOAA diving official for matters relating to the interpretation and application of the NOAA diving regulations, policies, and procedures.

NOAA Diving Safety Officer: Individual assigned by the Director OMAO to monitor the safe conduct of the NDP, provide advice to the NDCSB and senior NOAA Management on diving safety and health related issues, and manage and direct the DUSA Program.

NOAA Line/Staff Office Diving Officers: Individuals appointed to oversee and direct diving activities within specific NOAA Line/Staff offices and to serve on the NOAA Diving Control and Safety Board (NDCSB).

NOAA Scientific Diver: A diver who has been authorized by the Director of the NOAA Diving Program to conduct dives in support of NOAA's science activities.

NOAA Special Task Endorsement: A 12 month authorization granted to NOAA scientific divers by the LODO/SODO to perform underwater tasks other than those authorized in the NOAA Scientific Diving Standards and Safety Manual.

NOAA Standardized Equipment Program (SEP): The formalized system used by the NOAA Dive Program for the maintenance and distribution of diver-worn equipment issued to NOAA divers.

NOAA Unit Diving Supervisors: NOAA divers appointed by a NOAA Line/Staff Office (LO/SO) Diving Officer to oversee, direct, and approve diving activities conducted within their respective LO/SO unit and to administer to the needs of assigned divers.

NOAA Volunteer Divers: Individuals who perform diving services for NOAA on their own initiative without a formal request or compensation other than reimbursement for travel and minor expenses.

No-decompression Limits: A series of relationships between time and depth below which, either through a shallower depth or less time, a diver may make a safe direct ascent to the surface.

Normal Ascent: An ascent made with an adequate gas supply at a rate of 30 feet per minute or less.

Oxygen Clean: A physical condition of diving equipment in which all combustible contaminants have been removed.

Oxygen Compatible: A gas delivery system that has components (o-rings, valve seats, diaphragms, etc.) that is compatible with oxygen at a stated pressure and temperature.

Oxygen Service: A gas delivery system that is both oxygen clean and oxygen compatible.

OTU (Oxygen Tolerance Unit): One OTU is the degree of pulmonary oxygen toxicity produced by breathing 100 percent O2 continuously at a pressure of 1 atmosphere absolute (ATA) for 1 minute.

Oxygen Toxicity: Any adverse reaction of the central nervous system ("acute" or "CNS" oxygen toxicity) or lungs ("chronic," "whole-body," or "pulmonary" oxygen toxicity) brought on by exposure to an increased (above atmospheric levels) partial pressure of oxygen.

PO_2: Inspired partial pressure of oxygen, usually expressed in units of atmospheres absolute.

Pressure Related Injury: An injury resulting from pressure disequilibrium within the body

Pressure Vessel: See cylinder.

Proficiency Dives: Dives performed solely for the purpose of maintaining previously acquired diving skills.

PSI (Pounds per Square Inch): A measurement of pressure which does not include the pressure of the atmosphere. PSI at the earth's surface is zero.

PSIG (Pounds per Square Inch Gauge): A measurement of pressure which includes ambient pressure.

Reciprocity Divers: Non-NOAA divers, employed by organizations, agencies, and institutions with which NOAA has established official agreements for the purpose of conducting collaborative diving operations.

Recompression Chamber: See decompression chamber.

Reserve Air Supply System (RASS): A diver-carried auxiliary supply of air, Nitrox, or mixed gas (as appropriate) sufficient under standard operating conditions to allow the diver to reach the surface, or another source of breathing gas, or to be reached by a standby diver.

Scientist: Individual who utilizes scientific expertise to perform scientific dives without direct or indirect supervision or guidance from a more qualified individual as determined by the on-site Divemaster/Lead Diver and Chief Scientist.

Scientific Dives: Dives performed solely as a necessary part of a scientific, research, or education activity by individuals whose sole purpose for diving is to perform scientific or research tasks for the advancement of science.

Scientist In-Training: Individual who utilizes scientific expertise to perform scientific dives under the direct or indirect supervision or guidance of a scientist and approval of the on-site Divemaster or Lead Diver.

SCUBA Diving: A diving mode independent of surface supply in which the diver uses self contained underwater breathing apparatus.

NOAA Staff Office Diving Officer: Individual appointed to oversee and direct diving activities within OMAO and to serve on the NOAA Diving Control and Safety Board (NDCSB).

Standby Diver: A diver at the dive location appropriately equipped and able to enter the water to assist a diver within one minute.

Surface Supplied Diving: A diving mode where the breathing gas is supplied from the surface by means of a pressurized umbilical hose. The umbilical generally consists of a gas supply hose, strength member, pneumofathometer hose, and communication line.

Training Dives: Dives performed solely for the purpose of acquiring new, or relearning previously acquired, diving skills.

Umbilical: Composite hose bundle between a dive location and a diver or bell, or between a diver and a bell, which supplies a diver or bell with breathing gas, communications, power, and/or heat, as appropriate to the diving mode or conditions, and includes a safety line between the diver and the dive location.

Working Dives: Underwater tasks that fall outside the Occupational Safety and Health Administration scientific exemption that do not require scientific expertise, may not lead to the advancement of science and involve tools and techniques beyond those required to perform scientific dives.

Working Pressure: Normal pressure at which a system is designed to operate.

NOAA DIVING PROGRAM - DIVE OPERATIONS PLAN

Date(s) of Operations:		Time of Operations:	
Location of Operations:		Number of Divers:	
Distance from Shore:		Planned # of Dives per Day:	
Evac. Time to Chamber:		Max Possible # of Dives to be Logged/Day:	
Depth Range of Dive Ops:		Number of Consecutive Dive Days:	
Platform:		On-Duty Dive ☐ Off-Duty Dive w/SEP gear ☐	

Scientific Dive (meets all criteria) ☐ Working Dive ☐	Float Plan Required	Yes ☐ No ☐	Safe Ship Checklist Required	Yes ☐ No ☐

Diving Mode:	SCUBA ☐ Surface Supplied ☐	Decompression Calculation Method:	Dive Computer ☐ Decompression Tables ☐

Divemaster / Lead Diver:

Divers:

Purpose of dives and tasks to be performed:

Principal Diver-Worn Equipment & Breathing Media:

Tools / Specialized Equipment to be Used: Tethered comms dive? ☐ Yes ☐ No

Potential Hazards & Mitigations:

Certain hazards are present on all dives (AGE, DCS, drowning, etc.), the above are unique to this operation.

Primary means of Evacuation for Emergencies:

Submitted by: (Print)	Signature:	Date:
Reviewed by: (Print) UDS or Designee	Signature:	Date:

Revised: 9 November 2011

Date: _____

NOAA DIVING PROGRAM
DIVING EMERGENCY ASSISTANCE PLAN

NOAA Diving Unit and Dive Location:

Instructions

To be completed and submitted to NDP.Diveplans@noaa.gov with initial dive plan of each calendar year and every time any information in the Diving Emergency Assistance Plan changes.

General Procedures

A Evaluate victim's Airway, Breathing, and Circulation (ABCs).

B If not breathing, begin basic life support to include CPR if necessary. Use a Manually Triggered Ventilator (MTV) or bag-type oxygen resuscitator.

C If breathing, place diver in supine position and administer 100% oxygen using a MTV/ demand oxygen resuscitator or nonrebreather type mask.

D If condition is life-threatening, call local Emergency Medical System (EMS) or USCG for transport to nearest medical treatment facility. If condition is not life-threatening, contact NOAA DMO for guidance. If unable to reach NOAA DMO within 15 min, contact Divers Alert Network.

E Keep victim comfortable and observe for shock or change in condition. If not nauseated and not experiencing altered level of consciousness, give victim water to drink.

F Gather additional information about the incident and prepare for transport.

G Call NOAA DMO, (206) 300-2098, (if not already done) to report incident.

Contacts

Primary Operational Recompression Chamber

Name:

Address:

Point of Contact:

Telephone Number:

Secondary Operational Recompression Chamber

Name:

Address:

Point of Contact:

Telephone Number:

Revised: 9 November 2011

Primary Hospital Emergency Room

Name:

Address:

Point of Contact:

Telephone Number:

Secondary Hospital Emergency Room

Name:

Address:

Point of Contact:

Telephone Number:

Shore-Based Emergency Transportation

Name:

Point of Contact:

Telephone Number:

At-Sea Emergency Transportation

Name:

Point of Contact:

Telephone Number:

Unit Diving Supervisor

Name:

Telephone Number:

Nearest U.S. Coast Guard Rescue Coordination Center:

- Great Lakes, East Coast and Gulf of Mexico:
    Atlantic Area Search and Rescue (SAR) Coordinator: (757) 398-6700
- Hawaii, Alaska, Pacific Coast:
    Pacific Area Search and Rescue (SAR) Coordinator: (510) 437-3700

NOAA DMO: CDR Joel Dulaigh   office (206) 526-6474   cell (206) 300-2098

NOAA DSO: Steve Urick   office (206) 526-6223   cell (206) 619-1615

Divers Alert Network: (919) 684-9111 or (800) 446-2671   Revised: 9 November 2011

NOAA DIVING PROGRAM
PRE AND POST DIVE CHECKLIST

PRE-DIVE

1. Mission Safety

☐ Dive objectives and goals are defined, reviewed and understood by the dive and support personnel.

☐ The Diving Accident Management Plan is posted, coordinated and reviewed (i.e., chamber availability, evacuation route, etc.), and all personnel are informed of their duties.

☐ Conduct a pre-dive briefing.

2. Evaluate and Prepare for Potential Hazards

☐ Identify dive site entry procedures and exit access point(s).

☐ Define depth, bottom time and cylinder ending pressure limits for the planned dive.

☐ Evaluate and discuss potential for entrapment, entanglement, other physical or mechanical hazards, bottom obstructions, dangerous bottom conditions or marine life, and marine traffic hazards.

☐ Complete Dive Safe Ship Operations (NOAA Form 64-3), if applicable.

3. Diving and Support Personnel

☐ Ensure that all divers are authorized to perform their assigned duties according to their NOAA certification levels (i.e., Working Diver, Scientific Diver, Trainee Diver, or Observational Diver).

☐ Ensure that all divers are qualified to complete assigned underwater tasks safely.

☐ Ensure support personnel understand all diver hand signals, emergency recall signals and can offer immediate assistance in case of an emergency.

☐ Provide an assessment of repetitive dive designations of a previous dive was made within 12 hours.

4. Equipment

☐ All support equipment (boats, compressor, oxygen kit, tools, etc.) are operated by trained personnel.

☐ All dive techniques to be used are safe and appropriate and authorized.

☐ All tools used are appropriate for the task.

☐ Complete diving first aid kit, first aid handbook, oxygen resuscitator, divemaster kit, a complete set of no-decompression air and Nitrox Tables, and dive flags are on site.

POST-DIVE

☐ Dive team buddies have remained together for a minimum of 30 minutes after each dive and have monitored each other's condition during that time.

☐ Notify watch on the vessel's bridge when operations are completed (if applicable).

☐ Ensure that all personal dive and support equipment is thoroughly cleaned and properly stowed.

☐ Conduct a dive debrief and critique operations, including procedures for flying after diving (if applicable).

Printed name of person completing checklist: _____

Signature of above person: _____

Date checklist completed: _____

RESCUE and DIVING SKILLS CHECKOUT REPORT

Name of Diver being evaluated: _____   Date: _____

Certification level: ☐ OBSERVER ☐ SCIENTIFIC ☐ WORKING ☐ ADVANCED WORKING ☐ MASTER

Name / location of Dive Unit: _____   Name of UDS: _____

Name of Diver conducting evaluation: _____   Signature: _____

PRELIMINARY OBSERVATIONS

Current training & medical: Gear present and in good working condition:

☐ Dive Physical   ☐ Regulator   ☐ Bottom Timer   ☐ Weight Belt/Harness   ☐ Snorkel
☐ CPR / AED   ☐ Alt. 2nd Stage   ☐ Dive Computer   ☐ Cylinder   ☐ Fins
☐ First Aid   ☐ Pressure Gauge   ☐ BCD   ☐ Mask   ☐ Knife
☐ Oxygen Administration   ☐ Depth Gauge   ☐ Wet/Dry Suit   ☐ RASS

DIVER SKILL EVALUATION

(Note as U = Unsatisfactory, N = Needs Improvement, S = Satisfactory, E = Excellent)

Physical fitness	_____	Ditch and don BCD _____
Swimming ability	_____	Weight belt removal / replacement _____
Properly weighted	_____	Disconnect / reconnect inflators (BCD/Dry Suit) _____
Buoyancy control	_____	V.V.D.S. roll outs & venting _____
Controlled descent / ascent rate	_____	Pre-dive buddy check _____
U/W communication (hand signals)	_____	Buddy contact and awareness during dive _____
U/W navigation & orientation	_____	Buddy breathing _____
Mask removal, replace & clear	_____	Deploy and use RASS for controlled ascent _____
Regulator recovery	_____	Recover unconscious diver from water _____

POST DIVE ASSESSMENT

Critique of
ability and
skills

Remarks or
problems
encountered

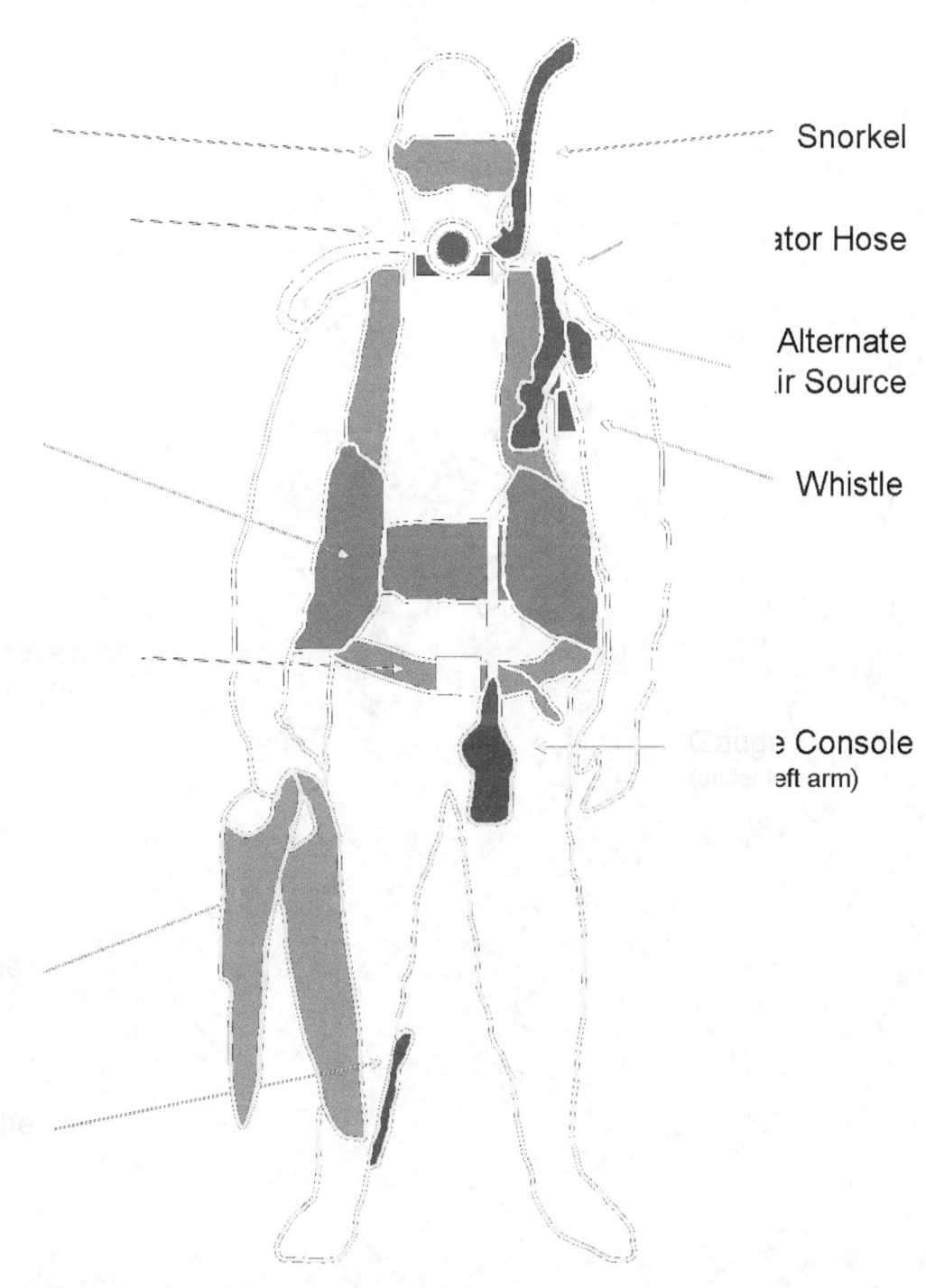

Snorkel

ator Hose

Alternate
ir Source

Whistle

Gauge Console
(under left arm)

Fins

Knife

S

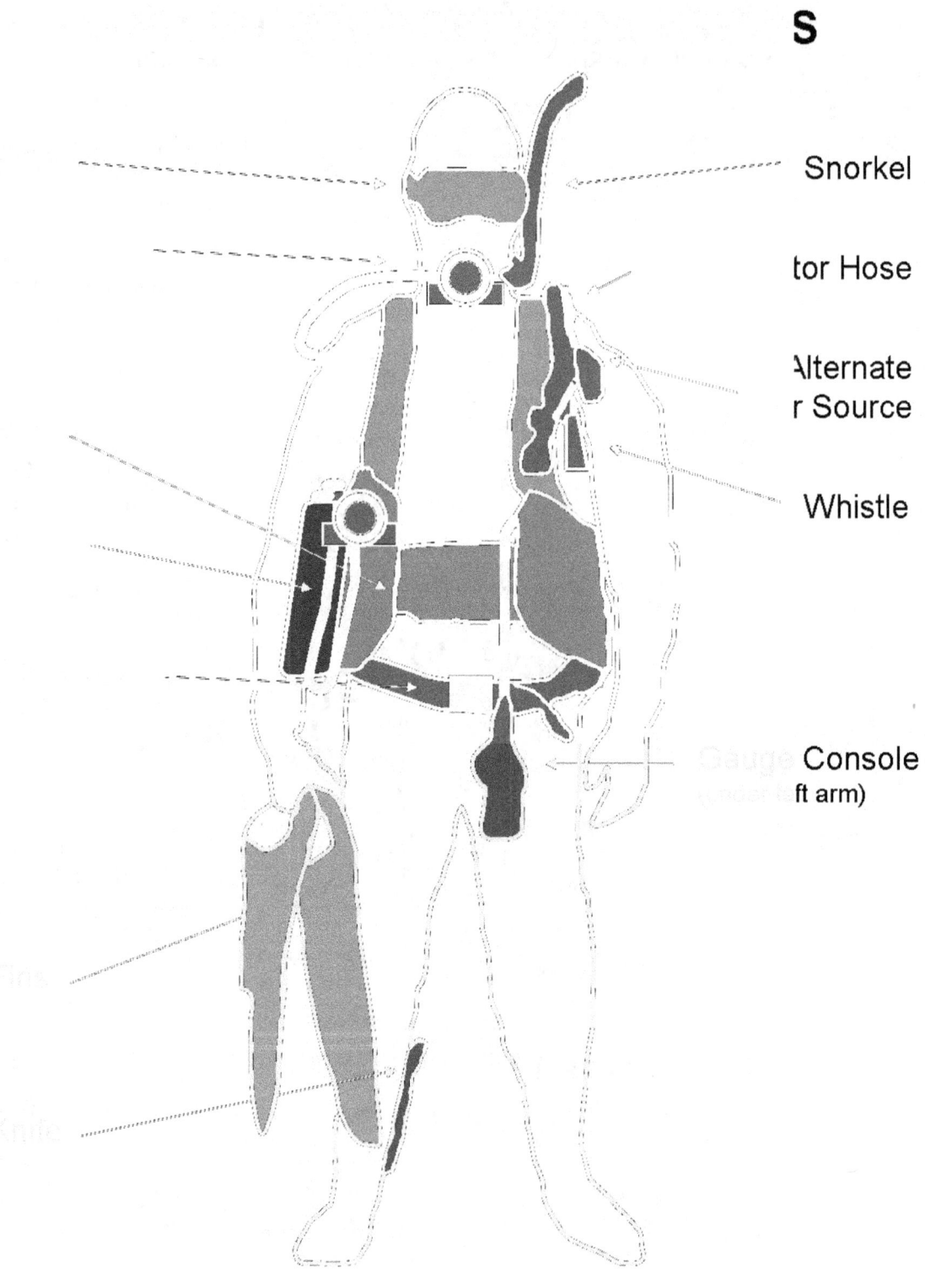

Snorkel

tor Hose

Alternate
r Source

Whistle

Console
ft arm)

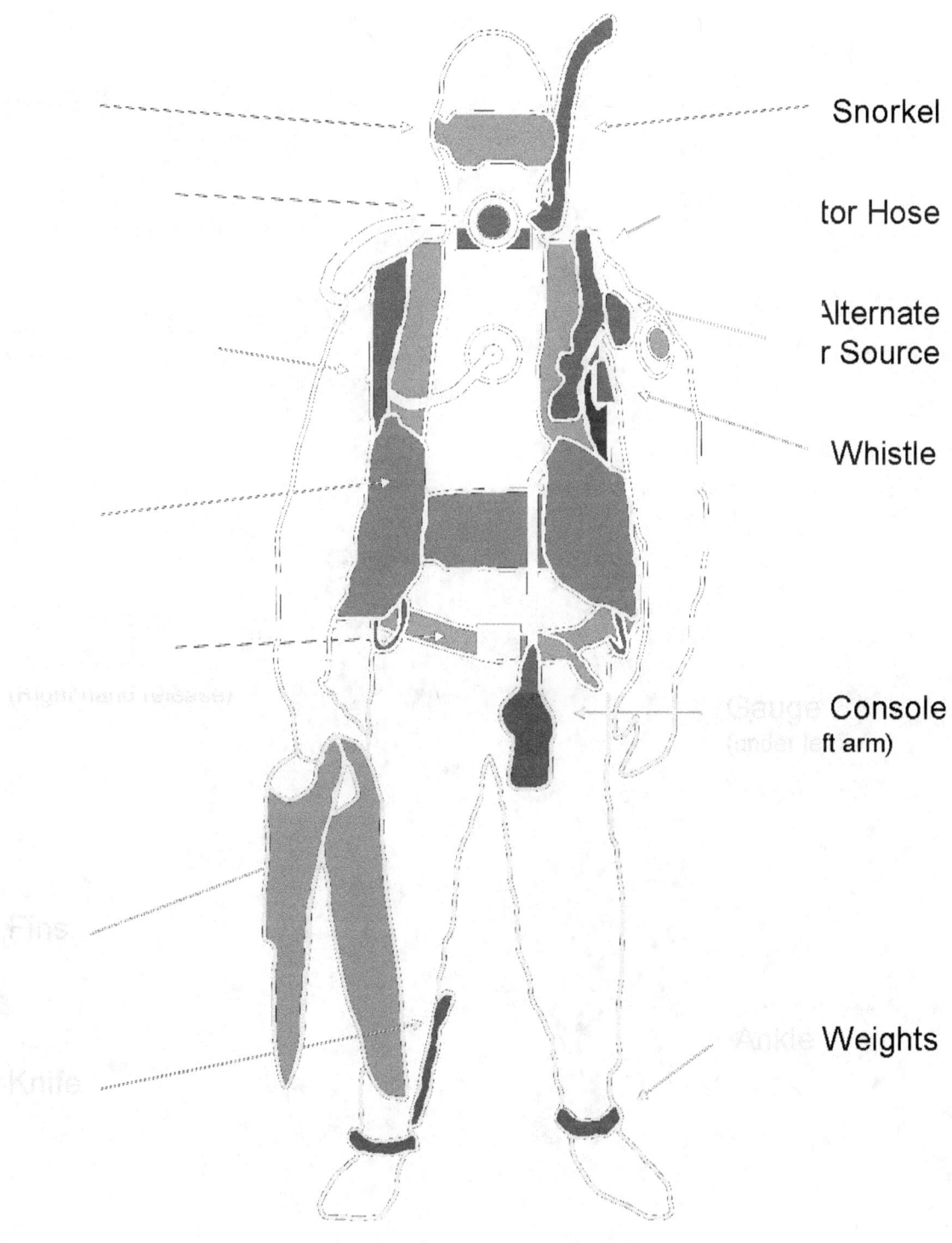

Snorkel

tor Hose

Alternate
r Source

Whistle

Console
(under left arm)

Weights

Fins

Knife

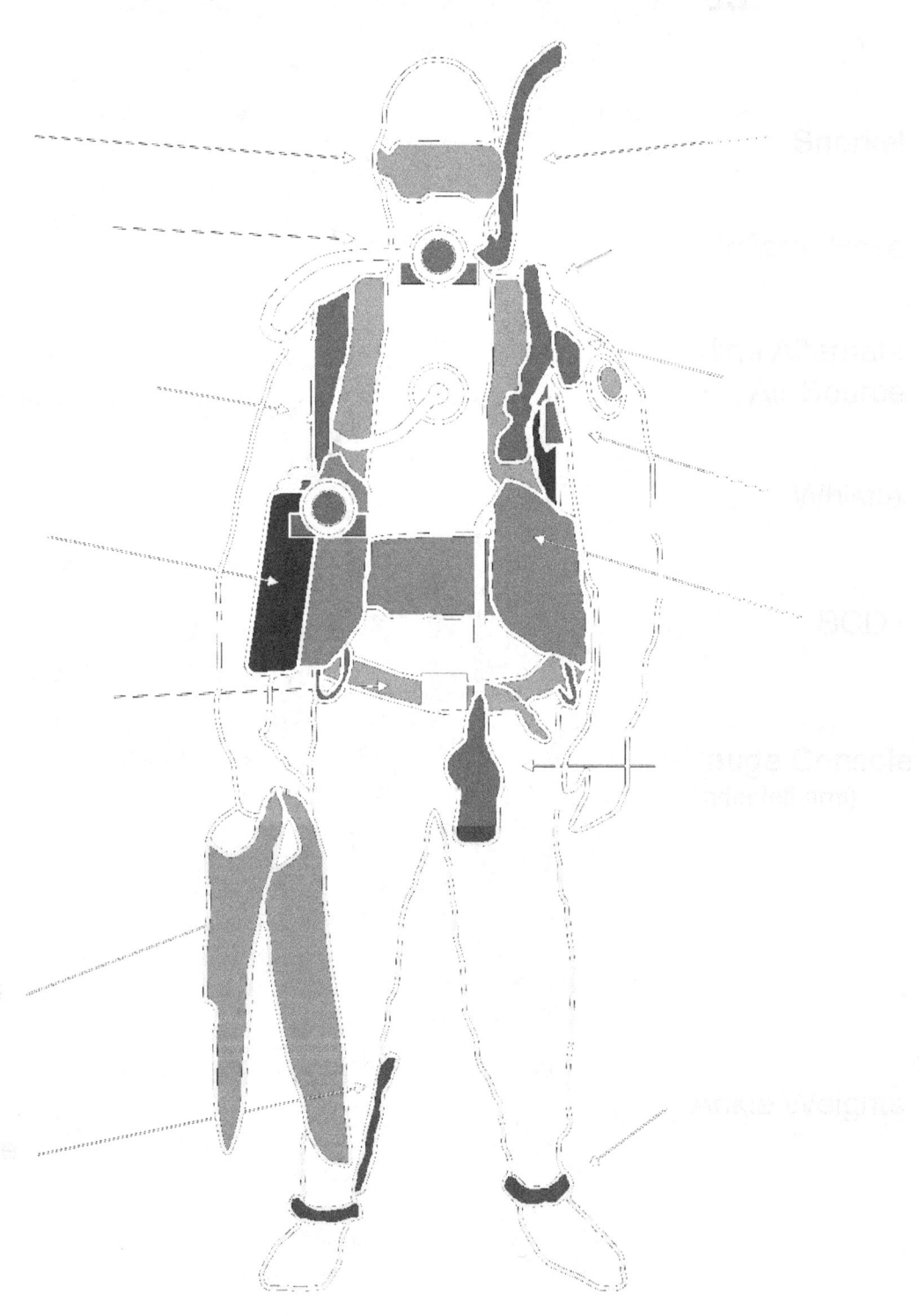

APPENDIX 8

NDP DIVE PLAN REVIEW POLICY ALGORITHM

Instructions: The algorithm to the right is intended to address the potential dangers of moderately deep, multi-day, multi-dive operations from a safety perspective. It is intended to help ensure that appropriate safeguards are in place to protect NOAA personnel engaged in remote diving operations.

An answer of 'yes' to each of the four decision boxes will necessitate submission of the NOAA Diving Center – Dive Operations Planning Sheet to the appropriate LODO/SODO for review. The LODO/SODO will review the information and determine if any special safety precautions are needed, including an on-site hyperbaric chamber.

Any 'no' answers will negate the need for review of the dive plan.

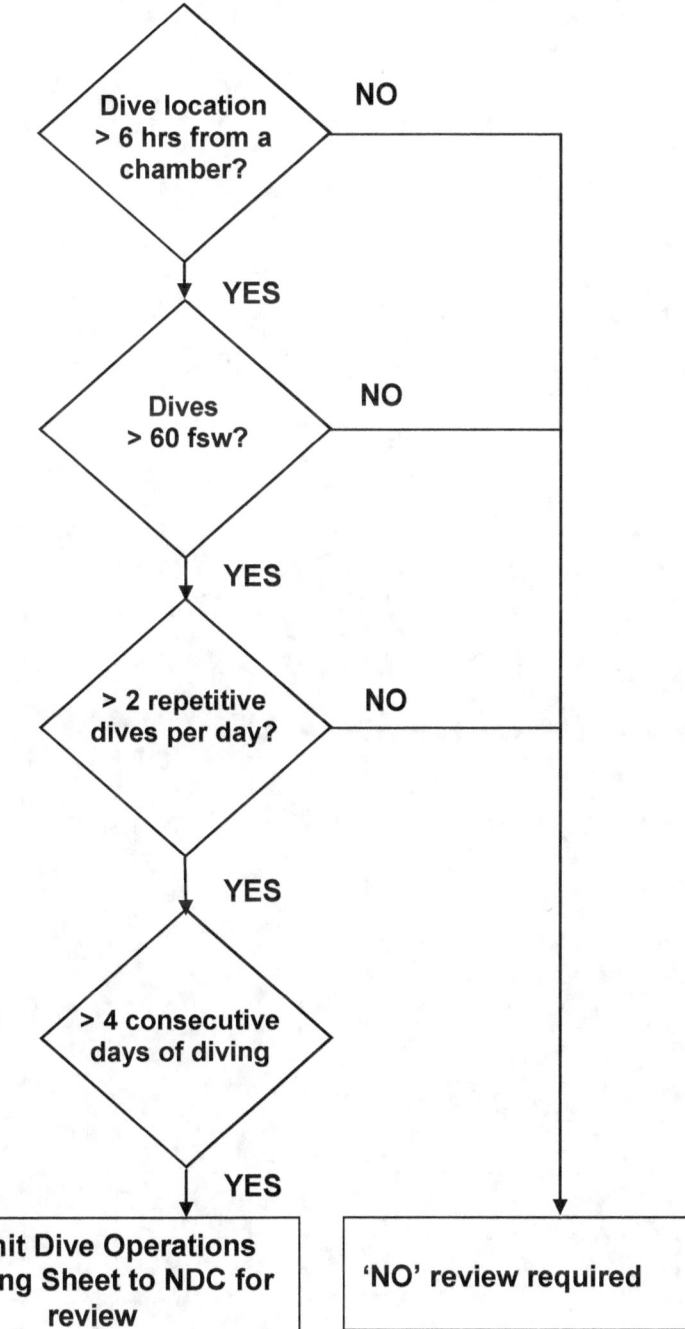

Dive location > 6 hrs from a chamber? — NO

YES

Dives > 60 fsw? — NO

YES

> 2 repetitive dives per day? — NO

YES

> 4 consecutive days of diving

YES

Submit Dive Operations Planning Sheet to NDC for review

'NO' review required

APPENDIX 9

NOAA DIVERS FIRST AID KIT INVENTORIES

NOAA DIVERS FIRST AID KIT INVENTORY – SMALL KIT

General Items
DAN First Aid pocket book
Laminated Diver Injury report form w/ grease
  pencil
DMT Neuro exam slate
Inventory checklist slate
Pencil
Latex free gloves (12 pair)
Pocket mask
Tongue depressors
Oral airway

Dressing pack
Band aids – 1x3" (20)
Bacitracin or double antibiotic ointment (6)
Gauze 2X2s (5)
Gauze 4X4 dressings (5)
Non-stick (Telfa) dressings (3)
Gauze 2" roller bandage (2)
Gauze 4" roller bandage (2)
8X10 Abd dressing (2)
1" tape (2 rolls)
Silicon tape (1)
Cotton tip applicators – sterile (2)
Alcohol prep pads (12)
Chlorhexidine packets (10)
E-Z Scrub brush with chloroxylenol (1)
20cc syringe for irrigation

Drug Pack
Ibuprofen Tablets, 200mg (10)
Acetaminophen 500mg (10)
Diphenhydramine 25 mg (10)
Antacids
Loperamide (10)
Burn Jel packets (6)

Orthopedic Pack
Sam Splint (1)
Cold Compress (1)
Triangular bandages (2)
2" cloth tape (1 rolls)
3" Ace wrap (2)

Diagnostics/tools
Scissors (EMT shears)
Ring cutter
Tweezers
Small water resistant flashlight
Pint size bottle vinegar

NOAA DIVERS FIRST AID KIT INVENTORY – LARGE KIT

General Items
DAN First Aid pocket book
Laminated Diver Injury report form w/ grease
    pencil
DMT Neuro exam slate
Inventory checklist slate
Pen/pencil
Non latex gloves (12 pair)
Face shield with mask
Pocket mask
Tongue depressors (3)
Oral airways (1 each adult sizes)

Dressing pack
Band aids – 1x3" strip type (20)
Band aids – knuckle (5)
Bacitracin or double antibiotic ointment (10)
Adaptic non-adhering dressing (3)
Opsite transparent dressing (3)
Gauze 2X2s (10)
Gauze 4X4 dressings (5)
Non-stick (Telfa) dressings (5)
Kerlix 4" roll (2)
Gauze 2" roller bandage (4)
Gauze 4" roller bandage (4)
8X10 Abd dressing (2)
10X30 Trauma dressing (1)
Clot activator impregnated dressings (4)
1" tape (3 rolls)
Silicon tape
Steri strips (0.25" x 1.5")
Benzoin ampules (10)
Cotton tip applicators – sterile (5)
Alcohol prep pads (20)
Chlorhexidine packets (10)
E-Z Scrub brush with chloroxylenol (2)
20cc syringe for irrigation

Orthopedic Pack
Sam Splint (1)
Short board splint (1)
Cold Compress (2)
Triangular bandages (4)
2" cloth tape (1 roll)
3" Ace wrap (4)

Drug Pack
Ibuprofen Tablets, 200mg (20)
Acetaminophen 500mg (20)
Diphenhydramine 25 mg (20)
Antacids
Loperamide (20)
Hydrocortisone Cream, 1%, 1.5g
Burn Jel packets (6)

Diagnostics/tools
Blood pressure cuff
Stethoscope
Small water resistant flashlight
Thermometer
Scissors (EMT shears)
Reflex hammer
Ring cutter
Tweezers
Pocket Otoscope
Quart size bottle vinegar
Disposable razor (3)

APPENDIX 10

NOAA SCIENTIFIC DIVER SKILLS CHECKLIST

Student Name: _____ LO/Unit: _____

Instructor Name: _____ LO/Unit: _____

SKILLS	PASS	DATE
Training Session One (Pool)		
1. Swim 550 yards[1]		
2. Swim 25 yards underwater[2]		
3. Tread water for 30 minutes on surface[3]		
Training Session Two (Pool)		
1. Equipment setup and donning with buddy[4]		
2. Pre-dive safety check[4]		
3. Giant stride entry[6]		
4. Forward roll entry[6]		
5. Backward roll entry[6]		
6. Controlled seated entry[1]		
7. Adjust weight[6]		
8. Regulator – snorkel exchange while swimming[1]		
9. Descent[6]		
10. Ascent[6]		
11. Remove, replace and clear mask[6]		
12. Remove, recover and replace regulator using reach method[6]		
13. Remove, recover and replace regulator using sweep method[6]		
14. Remove, recover and replace regulator using tank lift method[6]		
15. Remove and replace weight belt underwater[6]		
16. Remove and replace scuba unit underwater[3]		
17. Remove and replace WB at surface		
18. Remove and replace BCD at surface		
19. Share air with alternate air source inflator (donor)[6]		
20. Share air with alternate air source inflator (receiver)[6]		
21. Buddy breathe (donor)[6]		
22. Buddy breathe (receiver)[6]		
23. Controlled emergency swimming ascent (diagonal)[6]		
24. Controlled emergency swimming ascent (vertical)[6]		
25. Buoyant emergency swimming ascent simulation (vertical)[6]		
26. Self rescue using RASS[6]		
27. Runaway BCD/drysuit inflator response[5]		
28. No mask drills[2]		
29. Breathing from freeflow regulator		
30. Air turned off drill		
31. Water exit[1]		
32. Equipment shutdown, disassembly and maintenance[1]		
Training Session Three (Confined/Open-Water)		

SKILLS	PASS	DATE
1. Equipment setup and donning with buddy[1]		
2. Pre-dive safety check[1]		
3. Water entry[5]		
4. Buoyancy check and proper weighting[6]		
5. Regulator – snorkel exchange while swimming[1]		
6. Descent[6]		
7. Ascent[6]		
8. Neutral buoyancy at depth[6]		
9. Remove, replace and clear mask[6]		
10. Remove, recover and replace regulator[6]		
11. Remove and replace scuba unit[6]		
12. Remove and replace weight belt underwater[6]		
13. Share air with alternate air source inflator (donor)[6]		
14. Share air with alternate air source inflator (receiver)[6]		
15. Buddy breathe (donor)[6]		
16. Buddy breathe (receiver)[6]		
17. Controlled emergency swimming ascent from <30 feet		
18. Self rescue using RASS[6]		
19. Remove and replace weight belt on surface[3]		
20. Remove and replace scuba unit[3] on surface		
21. Water exit[1]		
22. Equipment shutdown, disassembly and maintenance[1]		
Training Session Four		
1. Equipment setup and donning with buddy[1]		
2. Pre-dive safety check[1]		
3. Water entry[6]		
4. Assist a tired diver[3]		
5. Assist a panicked diver[3]		
5. Assist a panicked diver[6]		
6. Assist unconscious diver[3]		
7. Assist unconscious diver[6]		
8. Tow and perform in-water rescue breathing for unconscious diver[3]		
9. Extricate an unconscious diver from the water[3]		

[1] Skill performed at surface
[2] Skill performed underwater (any depth)
[3] Skill performed at surface in water depth too deep to stand in
[4] Skill perform on the surface (e.g., pool deck, pier, vessel)
[5] Skill performed in water depth shallow enough to stand in
[6] Skill performed in water depth too deep to stand in

The above named individual has satisfactorily demonstrated all the skills listed per criteria outlined in the NOAA Scientific Diver Instructor Guide.

Instructor Signature: _____Date: _____

APPENDIX 11

NOAA SCIENTIFIC DIVER TRAINING COURSE
STUDENT EVALUATION RECORD

Student Name: _____ _____ ____
                            Last   First   MI

Prerequisites

Requirements	✓
Training request approved by supervisor	
Diving physical approved by NDP DMO	
Copies of Scuba certification	
Copies of current CPR, First Aid, AED and oxygen delivery training	
Copy of diver resume verifying minimum logged dives	

Final Written Examinations (minimum 80% required)

Subject	Exam A/B	Score	Date
Physics			
Physiology			
Hazardous Aquatic Life			
Equipment			
Standards and Regulations			
Diving Skills and techniques			
Dive Planning and USN Dive Tables			

Water Skills

Skill	Pass	Date
Swim evaluation		
Basic scuba skills (pool)		
Basic scuba skills (open-water)		
Rescue skills (pool)		
Rescue skills (open-water)		

The above named individual has satisfactorily demonstrated the skills and knowledge required by the NOAA Diving Program for certification as a NOAA Scientific Diver.

Instructor Name: _____ _____
                              Last   First

Instructor Signature: _____ Date: _____

APPENDIX 12

NOAA DIVING ACCIDENT MANAGEMENT FLOWCHART

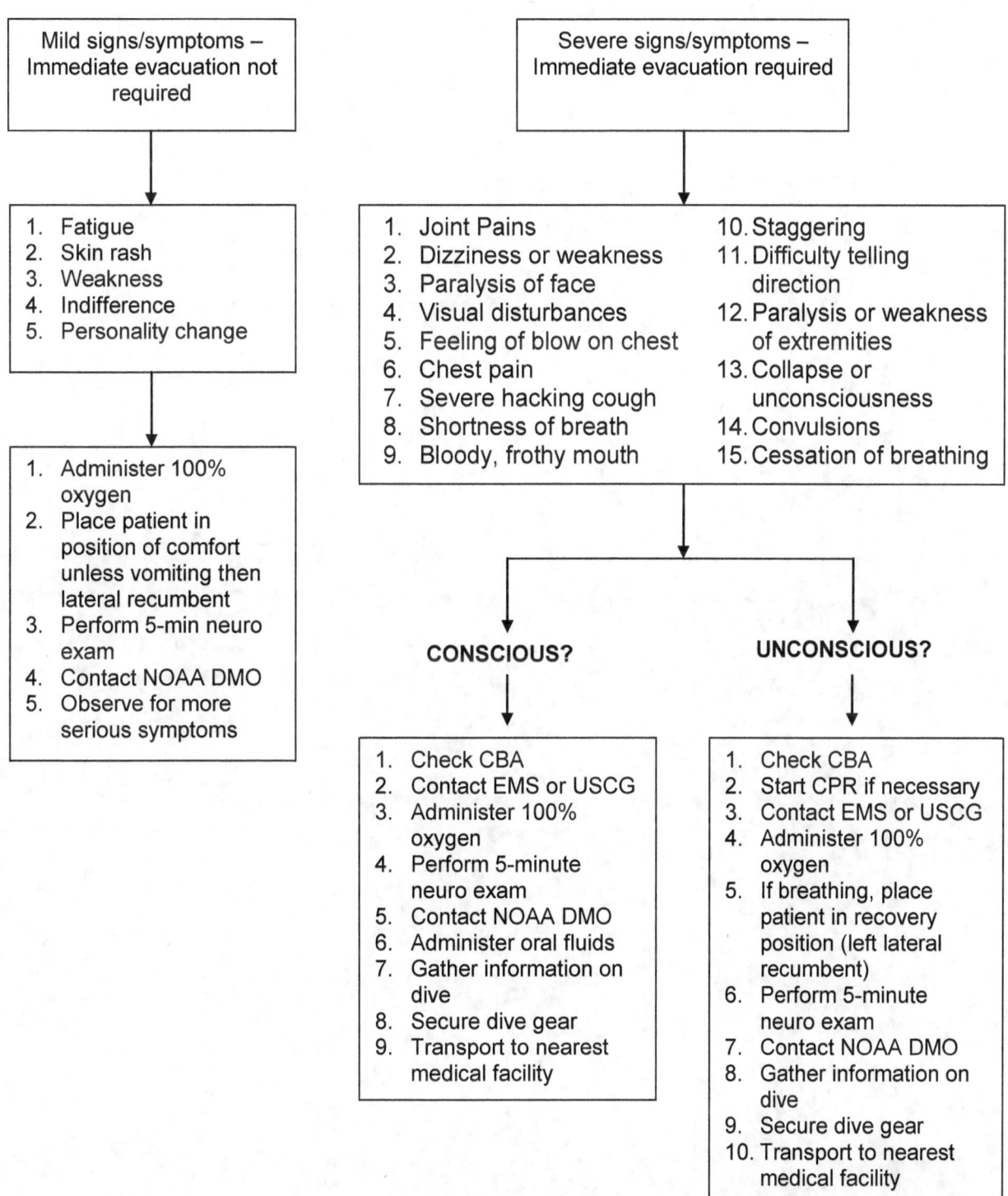

Mild signs/symptoms – Immediate evacuation not required

1. Fatigue
2. Skin rash
3. Weakness
4. Indifference
5. Personality change

1. Administer 100% oxygen
2. Place patient in position of comfort unless vomiting then lateral recumbent
3. Perform 5-min neuro exam
4. Contact NOAA DMO
5. Observe for more serious symptoms

Severe signs/symptoms – Immediate evacuation required

1. Joint Pains
2. Dizziness or weakness
3. Paralysis of face
4. Visual disturbances
5. Feeling of blow on chest
6. Chest pain
7. Severe hacking cough
8. Shortness of breath
9. Bloody, frothy mouth
10. Staggering
11. Difficulty telling direction
12. Paralysis or weakness of extremities
13. Collapse or unconsciousness
14. Convulsions
15. Cessation of breathing

CONSCIOUS?

1. Check CBA
2. Contact EMS or USCG
3. Administer 100% oxygen
4. Perform 5-minute neuro exam
5. Contact NOAA DMO
6. Administer oral fluids
7. Gather information on dive
8. Secure dive gear
9. Transport to nearest medical facility

UNCONSCIOUS?

1. Check CBA
2. Start CPR if necessary
3. Contact EMS or USCG
4. Administer 100% oxygen
5. If breathing, place patient in recovery position (left lateral recumbent)
6. Perform 5-minute neuro exam
7. Contact NOAA DMO
8. Gather information on dive
9. Secure dive gear
10. Transport to nearest medical facility

APPENDIX 13
NOAA DIVE INCIDENT REPORTING PROCEDURES AND TIMELINE

Immediate Actions

Follow-up Actions

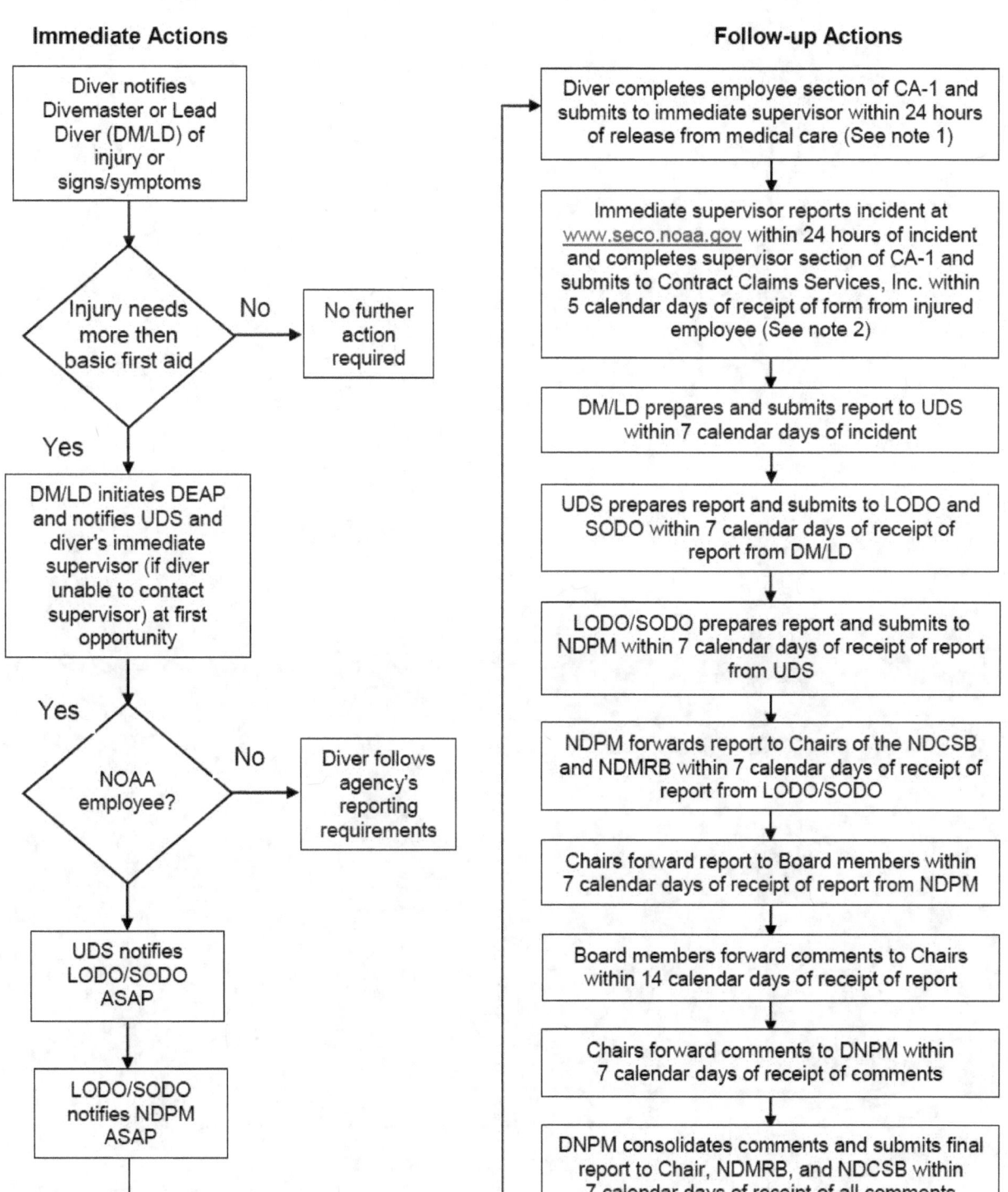

Diver notifies Divemaster or Lead Diver (DM/LD) of injury or signs/symptoms

Injury needs more then basic first aid → No → No further action required

Yes

DM/LD initiates DEAP and notifies UDS and diver's immediate supervisor (if diver unable to contact supervisor) at first opportunity

Yes

NOAA employee? → No → Diver follows agency's reporting requirements

UDS notifies LODO/SODO ASAP

LODO/SODO notifies NDPM ASAP

Diver completes employee section of CA-1 and submits to immediate supervisor within 24 hours of release from medical care (See note 1)

Immediate supervisor reports incident at www.seco.noaa.gov within 24 hours of incident and completes supervisor section of CA-1 and submits to Contract Claims Services, Inc. within 5 calendar days of receipt of form from injured employee (See note 2)

DM/LD prepares and submits report to UDS within 7 calendar days of incident

UDS prepares report and submits to LODO and SODO within 7 calendar days of receipt of report from DM/LD

LODO/SODO prepares report and submits to NDPM within 7 calendar days of receipt of report from UDS

NDPM forwards report to Chairs of the NDCSB and NDMRB within 7 calendar days of receipt of report from LODO/SODO

Chairs forward report to Board members within 7 calendar days of receipt of report from NDPM

Board members forward comments to Chairs within 14 calendar days of receipt of report

Chairs forward comments to DNPM within 7 calendar days of receipt of comments

DNPM consolidates comments and submits final report to Chair, NDMRB, and NDCSB within 7 calendar days of receipt of all comments

Note 1: Not applicable to NOAA Corps Officers
Note 2: Incidents occurring on NOAA Ships are to be reported using MOC-137

APPENDIX 14

DESCRIPTION OF NOAA SAFETY AND ENVIRONMENTAL COMPLIANCE OFFICE INCIDENT CLASSIFICATIONS

Class A Incident (NOAA Level Incident Investigation)

Injury to individuals	• Death from an incident; • 3 or more in-patient hospitalizations within 30 days from an incident; or • Incident involving permanent employee disability.
Dollar Loss	• Property damage or loss estimated at greater than $1,000,000.
Environmental Damage	• Release of a listed environmental pollutant in a quantity greater than, or equal to, the chemicals "Reportable Quantity (RQ)"; or • Release of an environmental pollutant outside of the boundaries of a NOAA Facility that requires notification and a clean-up response in accordance with applicable regulations.
Other	• Incident involving conditions that could pose an imminent and severe threat of serious injury to employees or the environment. • Loss of aircraft while flying. • Any incident elevated from a "Class B Mishap" by request, due to concerns by the investigation authority.

Class B (Line Office Level Incident Investigation)

Injury to individuals	• Any incident which results in an in-patient stay for an employee. • Injuries which result in five or more, consecutive, lost work days immediately following the incident. • Incident involving permanent partial disability. • Illness, upon the report of treatment, filing a CA-2, or a report of a suspect illness that will trigger further study.
Dollar Loss	• Property damage or loss estimated at greater than $20,000 but less than $1,000,000.
Environmental Damage	• Release of an environmental pollutant approaching the RQ.
Other	• Any Aircraft related incident that forces grounding of the aircraft. • Loss of vessel while underway regardless of size that does not result in a Class A Mishap. • Near miss incidents of nationwide significance reported via NOAA reporting system or Commerce Department (CD) form CD 351. • Any incident elevated from a "Class C Mishap" by request, due to concerns by the investigation authority.

Class C (Supervisor or Designee Level Incident Investigation)

Injury to individuals	• Any incident which causes an injury. • Incidents which involve first aid medical treatment. • Incidents which result in an employee being taken to a hospital emergency room, without requiring an in-patient stay.
Dollar Loss	• Property damage or loss up to $20,000.
Environmental Damage	• Unintentional release of materials to the secondary containment.
Other	• Incidents involving contamination of personnel or environmental exposure by a potentially harmful substance; with no symptoms or circumstances that trigger other mishap classification. • Incidents or exposures that have caused concerns to workers or our customers to include near miss incidents of local significance reported via NOAA reporting system or on CD 351. • "Close-call" Incidents which had the potential to result in damages described above in "Class A Mishap" but do not trigger investigation elsewhere in this table. • All motor vehicle incidents, when investigated by law enforcement officials.

APPENDIX 15

NOAA DIVING PROGRAM
ANNUAL WATERMANSHIP ASSESSMENT

Candidate Name: _____ Date of Test: _____

Please verify the above individual's execution of the NOAA Annual Watermanship Assessment. Per the NOAA Diving Standards and Safety Manual, NOAA divers must pass this assessment on an annual basis to maintain active dive status.

<u>Minimum Requirements:</u>

1. Swim 550 yards (500 meters) without stopping using masks, fins, and snorkel in less than <u>10 minutes</u>.

2. If using a wetsuit covering any part of the torso, the test must be completed in less than <u>12 minutes</u>.

Time required to complete swim: _____ <u>with</u> or <u>without</u> a wetsuit (circle one)

Candidate   ☐ <u>met</u> minimum requirements (passed)
              ☐ <u>did not meet</u> minimum requirements (failed)

Candidate Signature _____

Evaluator Name _____

UDS or designee Signature _____

Organization/Unit: _____

This form shall be completed, signed and filed on site at the diver's unit.

www.ingramcontent.com/pod-product-compliance
Lightning Source LLC
Chambersburg PA
CBHW08025329052
45790CB00005B/1795